CHOPIN

AN INDEX OF HIS WORKS

CHOPIN

AN INDEX OF HIS WORKS
IN CHRONOLOGICAL ORDER

MAURICE J. E. BROWN

Second, Revised Edition

MACMILLAN

© Maurice J. E. Brown 1960, 1972

First edition 1960
Second edition 1972

Published by
THE MACMILLAN PRESS LTD
London and Basingstoke
Associated companies in New York Toronto
Dublin Melbourne Johannesburg and Madras

SBN 333 13535 0

Printed in Great Britain by
ROBERT MACLEHOSE AND CO LTD
The University Press, Glasgow

To the memory
of
ARTHUR HEDLEY

CONTENTS

FOREWORD TO THE FIRST EDITION

THIS book has been written to fill a gap in the Chopin literature. There is no lack, in fact there is a superfluity, of books dealing with the aesthetic approach to the works of the Polish composer, and with the interpretation of his works; there are several good, albeit incomplete, biographies of the man; there is one outstanding book containing full details of the bibliographical literature, by Bronisław Sydow. But of books devoted to a basic survey of Chopin's works, providing all known details of composition and publication, there is none.

I have gone to original sources, wherever possible, to obtain these details. The only reason why I have not produced the discovered information with the title 'Thematic Catalogue' is that I have no wish to suggest that Chopin's compositions stand in any need of a catalogue number, and certainly no desire that each of his works should be labelled with an initial and a number, as those of Mozart and Schubert have been. In their cases it is essential, and the Köchel and Deutsch numbers supply a vital need. Chopin's opus numbers are a quite reliable guide to chronology, and are, in themselves, perfectly adequate for identification purposes.

But for the student, performer or critic of Chopin, to say nothing of the librarian, bookseller or collector, there is no ready means of reference to his individual works. The Index to be found in the following pages not only presents a survey of his works, in chronological order, but also provides a ready and instantly obtained series of facts about each work.

These facts embody the dates and places of composition; the date of publication of all the first editions (and in the case of his mature works that means of the French, English and German editions); points of interest about the composition, publication or first performance of each work; and finally, the whereabouts, if it be known, of existing manuscripts.

There are many reasons why such a book as this Index has not hitherto been written. Chopin's background includes Poland, Austria and Germany, France and, to a certain degree, England – or perhaps Britain would be more accurate! The number of musicologists who can command Polish, German, English and French must be rather limited, and without all four of those languages Chopin research cannot be as thorough going as it should be. Imperfections in this Index are due to my elementary knowledge of Polish, and I have had either to use translations of Polish documents into German, or to rely on my own imperfect reading of the originals. Nevertheless, to wait until someone with a command of all four languages, together with the necessary musical knowledge, and a love for Chopin's music, *does* emerge, and undertakes the necessary sifting, might be to wait for a very long time, and however faulty the Index may be, it does at least make an effort to get the necessary studies started.

Another reason why this kind of book has not been compiled before, and which adds to the difficulties of a compiler today, is that Chopin seems not to have aroused the interest of bibliographers, particularly the industrious German bibliographers of the nineteenth century, to the same degree that the great German composers have done. The bibliographical source material for Chopin is considerably smaller than that for other composers of a comparable standing. It is surprising that whereas large, and sometimes complete, collections of the first editions of all the great composers can be found, not only in the larger national libraries of the world, but even in private possession, this is certainly not the case with Chopin. To give two examples: the British Museum possesses only an incomplete set of Wessel's English edition of Chopin, and the collection of French first editions of Chopin in the Bibliothèque Nationale, Paris, lacks several examples.

There are, of course, large collections of these first editions in private possession in Europe: for example, that of the late Arthur Hedley, London, and that of Mr Antony van Hoboken, Ascona. But these two collections are not complete; and in some cases, after a vain search, I have begun to wonder if a single copy of some of Chopin's first editions, e.g. of Chabal's publication of the 'Émile Gaillard' Mazurka, or of Kauffmann's edition of the E minor Waltz, is still extant anywhere in the world.[1] The unhappy experiences of Poland, in two world wars, have also led to the destruction of many such copies, as well as to the loss of autograph manuscripts.

The following list gives the more important catalogues of Chopin's works, which appeared between 1845 and 1954. Many of them are in order of opus numbers. The earlier ones are, understandably, incomplete and inaccurate, and the later ones, either by reason of brevity or because of subsequent discoveries, similarly unreliable. Mr Hedley's two catalogues are, it goes without saying, excellent, but in both of them reasons of space lead to the omission of full details, and neither of them, as he would have admitted, aims at completeness.

1. MS. Thematic Catalogue prepared for Jane Stirling by Chopin and Auguste Franchomme c. 1845. Later additions (by Sigismond von Neukomm?) continue the list to Op. 73, and beyond. Chopin wrote in his own hand Opp. 1, 37, 38, 48–50, 57 and 58. Only the first item is given for the sets of Studies in Opp. 10 and 25, and for the set of Preludes, Op. 28. The MS., which bears Jane Stirling's authentication, was reproduced in facsimile as a frontispiece to the *Oxford Edition of Chopin's Works*, vol. 1, London, 1932.

2. *Thematisches Verzeichniss der im Druck erschienenen Kompositionen von*

---

[1] I have been informed, since the above was written, that a copy of the 'Émile Gaillard' Mazurka is in the Muzeum Narodowa, Cracow.

Fr. Chopin. Breitkopf & Haertel, Leipzig, October 1852. Later issues, with additions, till *c.* 1870.

3. MS. List of the then unpublished works, prepared by Chopin's sister Louise (Ludwika), *c.* 1853 (probably for Fontana's projected publication of the posthumous works). Louise died in 1855, but someone in the family, her sister Isabella, or her daughter of the same name, added details – date, publisher, etc. – to the items as they were published. This list, known in the Index as 'Louise's list', was published for the first time in *Souvenirs inédits de Chopin,* 1904 (see Appendix IX).

4. *Thematisches Verzeichniss der im Deutschland erschienenen Instrumental-Kompositionen von Friedrich Chopin mit Beifügung der Textanfänge seiner Lieder,* by Dr Oscar Paul. It was a supplement to the *Musikalisches Wochenblatt* of 4 January 1870, published by Ernst Wilhelm Fritsch, Leipzig.

5. *Thematisches Verzeichniss der im Druck erschienenen Kompositionen von Fr. Chopin,* enlarged and revised, Breitkopf & Haertel, Leipzig, 1888.

6. *Stufenweise geordnete Verzeichniss sammtlicher Kompositionen von Fr. Chopin,* by Dr Hans Schmidt, Professor at the Conservatoire, Vienna. Later incorporated into the 1888 Catalogue above.

7. *Frederick Chopin as Man and Musician,* by Frederick Niecks, London, 1888, vol. II

8. *A Handbook to Chopin's Works,* by C. Ashton Johnson, Wm Reeves, London, 1905; rev. ed., 1908.

9. *Chopin,* by Arthur Hedley, J. M. Dent & Sons, London, 1946; rev. ed., 1963, pp. 187–93.

10. *Bibliografia F. F. Chopina,* by Bronisław Edward Sydow (Warsaw, 1949).

11. *Almanach Chopinowski 1949,* by Sydow (Warsaw, 1950).

12. 'Chopin', by Arthur Hedley, in *Grove's Dictionary,* 5th ed., Macmillan, London, 1954.

For each work in the Index I have quoted, in brackets, after the particular publisher the publisher's number (PN) of the first edition. These numbers, treated with care, constitute, in the words of Dr Otto Erich Deutsch, a 'new tool of bibliography', but it is a two-edged tool and can hardly ever be relied on, in isolation, for the purpose of dating a publication. In the case of Wessel, for example, it is clear that a whole batch of publisher's numbers was allotted to Chopin, to be used as, and when, Wessel acquired a new composition by him. Consecutive numbers, in Wessel's case, may indicate publications separated by several years.[1] In the same way, delayed publication of a work from Breitkopf & Haertel renders their publisher's number useless; contemporary advertisements are then the only reliable source of information.

It is by the aid of such advertisements that I have, in nearly all cases, obtained precise details of publication dates. In France and Germany, an unbroken sequence of advertisements in this or that periodical enables one to do so with accuracy; in England the lack of any musical periodical in the crucial years 1833–53[2] makes the task more difficult, but here the two bibliographical aids, Wessel's publisher's numbers and the acquisition dates on the copies of the first editions in the British Museum, taken in conjunction, help to bridge the gap. The famous *Verzeichniss der Musikalien* of Hofmeister is useful for German and Polish editions, and Senff, of Leipzig, issued a *Jahrbuch für Musik*, containing publications from Germany, Austria and Poland, between 1842 and 1852.

The eight posthumous works, Opp. 66–73, appeared in Berlin and Paris in 1855. They were edited – and that word has here some of its less desirable undertones – by Chopin's friend Julian Fontana. He obtained permission on 16 July 1853 from Chopin's family in Warsaw, that is, from his widowed mother Justina, and his sisters, Louise Jędrzejewski and Isabella Barcińska, to publish these works. They accordingly appeared under the title 'Œuvres Posthumes pour le piano de Fréd. Chopin publiés sur manuscrits originaux avec autorisation de sa famille par Jules Fontana'. He arranged them rather arbitrarily in categories, so that early mazurkes and waltzes jostle with

---

[1] See *Music and Letters*, London, October 1958.
[2] Since the above was printed several people have pointed out to me that there were (a)*The Musical Library* (1834–7) and (b) *Monthly Supplement to the Musical Library* (1834–6) in existence. This still leaves the main point above unanswered, since these periodicals were not in the same class as the later *Musical World* and *Musical Times*.

later ones, and wrote an uninformative preface, dated May
1855, introducing his edition. The eight sets of works were
published in Berlin with the opus numbers as we know them
and in Paris, by J. Meissonnier Fils, without opus numbers.
Fontana's prolonged negotiations with Breitkopf &
Haertel of Leipzig came to nothing; it is worth mention
that the German firm refused to publish these works on the
grounds of their inferiority! They did not appear in London
until many years had passed, although their copyright was
registered at Stationers' Hall in 1855. Both the French and
German editions contained as a frontispiece a portrait of
Chopin by Ary Scheffer (1795–1858), in Paris engraved by
Raunhim, in Berlin by Waldow. The final opus number,
Op. 74, comprising the sixteen (later seventeen) Polish
songs, appeared two years later, in 1857, and then only in
Germany.

The three editions of Chopin's works, published during
his lifetime in France, England and Germany, sometimes
give references to publishers in other countries, in Italy,
Belgium, Poland, Russia and so forth; these references have
been omitted in the Index whenever it was felt that the
firms specified were those only of agencies for the main
editions and not actual publishers of the works concerned.
Nor has it been possible to give details of all the republication during Chopin's lifetime of collections of his works in
similar forms, e.g. 'Complete Polonaises' or 'Complete
Impromptus'. In most cases the publisher merely bound
together the separate issues, or reused the original plates
giving the set a new title-page, and the pieces a consecutive
numbering.

The various appendices at the end of this book attempt to
give the Chopin student, in a concise and readily available
form, certain factual details which may be necessary to him
and to find which would entail a good deal of page-turning
in the biographies. In one case, that of the appendix devoted
to the poets of the songs, the information is not particularly

important but, as far as I know, appears nowhere else.
Wessel's English edition is listed in full, partly because the
Index is primarily addressed to English readers, and partly
because his numbering of the works does not follow the
opus numbering. The Bibliography is not intended to be a
complete one: I have included in it only such works as I
consider significant and relevant to this annotated Index.

Many people have helped me with the details of this book
and I cannot hope to mention them all individually. Chiefly
I am indebted to Mr Arthur Hedley, the eminent Chopin
scholar, whose collection of Chopiniana is unrivalled in the
world.[1] To Mr Antony van Hoboken I am almost as deeply
indebted for the many details of importance from his fine
collection of Chopin first editions. The third of my major
helpers is Mlle Simone Wallon, Assistant Librarian at the
Conservatoire de Musique, Bibliothèque Nationale, Paris;
I am most grateful for her valuable help in connection with
the collection of Chopin MSS. and first editions in that
library. Other librarians to whom my thanks are due are
Mlle B. Monkiewicz, of the Bibliothèque Polonaise, Paris;
Herr Dr F. Grasberger, of the Nationalbibliothek, Vienna;
and Mrs Hilda Andrews, of the Polish Cultural Institute,
London. Amongst other people who have made the preparation of this book possible, I should like to thank especi-
ally Mlles Suzanne and Denise Chainaye, the well-known
French authorities on Chopin; Dr Otto Erich Deutsch of
Vienna; Mr Adam Harasowski, the authority on Polish
folk-song; Mr Adam Rieger, editor of *Ruch Muzyczne*,
Cracow; and finally, M. Alfred Cortot, Lausanne, whose
kindness in providing details of the Chopin MSS. in his
possession is, alas, not too common amongst such fortunate
possessors.

In conclusion – an appeal to users of this book: I stress
once again my realisation that the Index has many imper-

---

[1] Most of Mr Hedley's MSS. were sold before his death to the Museo de Chopin,
La Cartuja, Valldemosa. The details appear in the necessary places in the Index.

fections and many gaps, inevitable is such a pioneering work. If its readers can supply any of these deficiencies, I should be grateful to hear of them.

M. J. E. B.

FOREWORD TO THE SECOND EDITION

THE plea at the close of the above Foreword has been generously answered and the revisions and enlargements in this new, revised edition of the Index are largely due to the work of those scholars who have written to me, correcting errors and adding new information and new discoveries. I am very grateful to Dr Adam Harasowski, who, with the lamented death of Arthur Hedley, now takes his place as one of the leading Chopin authorities in England. He has been responsible for the correction of errors in the Polish orthography which were a blemish on the first edition of the Index.

A scholar and bibliographer to whom I owe a great debt of thanks is Dr Alan Tyson, whose researches have straightened out the difficulties attendant on early publications (e.g. of Opp. 16 and 17) and have enabled me to correct publication dates of Wessel's English editions.

Other scholars who have helped me are Dr J. J. Fuld, of New York; Dr Ewald Zimmermann, of Duisburg; Ferdinand Gajewski, of Harvard University; Dr Julian Chochlow, of Moscow; and Mrs Barbara Henry, of New Orleans.

An article published in the *Musical Times* of January 1965 set out a number of the major corrections to the Index, now incorporated in the new edition. With the permission of the editor of that journal I am reproducing certain relevant material from that article, which cannot be so incorporated.

First Editions. The publisher's number (PN) given in the Index, in connection with the publication of each of Chopin's works, is the one that appears in the first edition. It does not follow, however, that every edition bearing this particular PN is accordingly a *first* edition. Editions of Chopin's early works, lithographed and published by Breitkopf & Haertel after the composer's death, may still bear the original PN; old plates, or – worse – new plates with the old numbers, were also used for decades. Collectors guided only by these original PNs would naturally be dismayed by finding on the back of a 'first edition' of, say, the Nocturnes, Op. 9, an advertisement for 'Ein Heldenleben'. The Index makes no claim to identify 'first editions' merely by its provision of the first PN.

Manuscripts. During the last few years it has been established that the small manuscript album containing seven songs and the Nocturne in C sharp minor (*Lento con gran espressione*) is not in the hand of Chopin, as was believed by scholars for over fifty years; it was written by his sister Louise. The album was intended by Chopin for Maria Wodzińska. Former attributions of various manuscripts to Chopin have now been corrected to 'Copy by Louise'. The MSS. in the Chopin Institute, Warsaw, are housed in the National Library (Bibliotheka Narodowa), Warsaw.

Publication dates. Entries in the registers of Stationers' Hall, London, and of the Dépôt Légal, Archives de France, Paris, have provided more accurate dates for several English and French publications. One general correction should be emphasised here: there seems no doubt that the 'Œuvres Posthumes', consisting of Opp. 66–73, were published in France on 28 July 1855 and not as late as suggested in the first edition of the Index.

MAURICE J. E. BROWN

Marlborough,
May 1970

POLONAISE in G minor. 1817

Publication:

> J. J. Cybulski, Warsaw (1882), November 1817.
> Republished in 1927 (see below).

Dedicated to Mlle la Comtesse Wiktoria Skarbek, daughter of Count Frederick Skarbek. Count Skarbek was a pupil of Nicolas Chopin, the composer's father.

The Polonaise, twenty-two bars long, with a sixteen-bar Trio in B flat major, was reviewed in a Warsaw literary periodical, *Pamiętnik Warszawski*, of January 1818, amongst a list of Polish books published in 1817. This review was known, but all trace of the music had disappeared. In 1924 a copy of it was found by Zdzisław Jachimecki of Cracow. He found it in some bound copies of piano pieces which had been published in Warsaw between 1816 and 1830. The four volumes of these bound pieces had belonged to the poet Josef Galuszka of Cracow. The copy of the Polonaise had been inscribed by Chopin himself 'Jan Białobłocki, writer'. A second copy was in the possession of Laura Ciechomska (a descendant of Chopin's sister, Louise) of Warsaw, whose collection was destroyed in 1939. A third copy is now in the possession of Antony van Hoboken, Ascona, Switzerland.

Jachimecki announced his discovery and republished the piece, in facsimile, in various musical periodicals of Europe, including the *Monthly Musical Record*, London, 1927. In 1947 he edited the Polonaise, together with the Polonaise in B flat (3) and the Polonaise in A flat (5) and the three were published as *Trzy Polonezy* ('Three Polonaises'): *1817–1821* by Krzyżanowski, S. A., Cracow.

The title-page of the Polonaise has been frequently reproduced in facsimile. The attribution is 'faite/par Frédéric Chopin/musicien âgé de huit ans/'.

(*a*) The 'Cracow' copy was reproduced in the *Monthly Musical Record*, March 1927. The words 'faite' and 'musicien' have been scratched out in this copy, possibly by Chopin himself.

(*b*) The 'Warsaw' copy was reproduced in Binental's *Documents*, Warsaw, 1930. It is unmarked in any way.

(*c*) On the 'Ascona' copy, only the word 'faite' is scratched out.

The Abbé Cybulski was the proprietor of a small music-printing business near St Mary's Church, Warsaw. Białobłocki (1805–28) was a boarder in the Chopin household (see note after **10** and also **17**).

MS. Lost.

2

MILITARY MARCH. 1817.

Publication:

1817, without the composer's name. No copy of this publication is known.

The March won the approval of the Grand Duke Constantine and on his orders was scored for military band (not by the composer) and performed for him in 1817.

MS. Lost.

3

POLONAISE in B flat major. 1817.

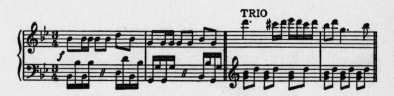

Publication:

    (*a*) A facsimile reproduction in *Kuryer Literacko-Naukowy*, Cracow, 22 January 1934.

    (*b*) A facsimile reproduction in the *Journal of the Frédéric Chopin Institute*, Warsaw, vol. 1, no. 1, 1937. Both facsimiles edited by Zdzisław Jachimecki.

The Polonaise, twenty bars long, with a sixteen-bar Trio in G minor, is known through a copy made by the composer's father, Nicolas, and inscribed: 'Polonaise pour le pianoforte composée par F. Chopin âgé 8 ans.' The copy was one of the autographs belonging to Alexander Poliński of Warsaw, the noted collector and historian of Polish music. After his death it passed into the State Collection, Warsaw, but was destroyed during the Second World War.

The work was identified as well as published by Jachimecki; he also edited it for publication in 1947 as the second of 'Three Polonaises' (see 1).

MSS. (1) Lost.

    (2) Nicolas Chopin's copy: destroyed.

    (3) Louise Chopin's copy: formerly with Arthur Hedley, London.

Lost works of the period:

    (*a*) A set of variations (mentioned in the *Pamiętnik Warszawski* of 1818).

(*b*) Two Polish dances presented by Chopin to the Empress Maria Teodorowna, mother of the Czar, on the occasion of her visit to Warsaw on 26 September 1818. One of these may have been the previous item.

4

MAZUREK (MAZURKA) in D major. (?) 1820.

Publication:

A facsimile reproduction in the *Kuryer*, Warsaw, no. 51, 20 February 1910, of a copy by an unknown writer.

The piece, thirty-four bars long, was part of the collection of autograph manuscripts belonging to Alexander Poliński (see **3**).

MS. Destroyed in the Second World War (it was formerly in the possession of the State Collection, Warsaw).

5

POLONAISE in A flat major. April 1821.

Publication:

Gebethner & Wolff, Warsaw (2515), 1902. This was from an unsatisfactory transcript made by Jan Micha-łowski.

Die Musik, Berlin, October 1908 (clean).

Dedicated to Wojciech (= Adalbert) Żywyny (1756–1842), Polish pianist and violinist, Chopin's first music-master.

The Polonaise, twenty-six bars long, with a thirteen-bar Trio in E flat major, was performed for Żywyny by Chopin on 23 April 1821. The manuscript, a doubtful autograph, was exhibited at the International Exhibition, Vienna, in 1892. It was reproduced in facsimile in *Chopin* (*Life and Work*), vol. 1, by Ferdinand Hoesick, Warsaw, 1910. For its republication as the third of 'Three Polonaises', see 1.

MS. Chopin Institute, Warsaw. If genuine, this is the earliest known manuscript of Chopin.

6

POLONAISE in G sharp minor. 1822.

Publication:

Josef Kauffmann, Warsaw (...), 1864.
B. Schott's Sons, Mainz (17, 943), 1864.

Dedicated to Mme (Sofie?) Dupont. The Duponts were

French friends of the composer's family. The marriage of one of Mme Dupont's daughters is mentioned by Chopin in his letter of 15 May 1830.

Niecks was of the opinion that the 'internal evidence of the work' pointed to a later date than 1822: the Gebethner edition (1878) is dated '1824'.

Kauffmann published the work in a series called 'Compositions modernes et classiques pour piano'. There were thirty-two pieces in the series, Chopin's 'Polonez' being 'No. 32'. No publisher's number is printed on the publication.

MS.   Lost.

7

MAZURKA in A flat major, Op. 7: no. 4 (first version). 1824.

Publication:

A facsimile reproduction is given in *Chopin in der Heimat*, Cracow, 1955, p. 84.

The Mazurka was written for the composer's schoolfriend, Wilhelm Kolberg (1809–77).

The manuscript bears, in the hand of Oskar, Wilhelm's brother, the words: 'Written by Fr. Chopin in the year 1824.' The section in D flat major is entitled by the composer on his manuscript 'Trio'.

For the final version, see **61**.

MS.   Society of Music, Warsaw.

8

MAZURKA in A minor, Op. 17: no. 4 (first version). August 1824.

This may be the work referred to by Chopin in the little mock newspaper (3 September 1824 'issue') which he and his sister Emilia devised for family reading and amusement in the summer of 1824 from Szafarnia (the 'Szafarnian Courier'). He reported '. . . M. Pichon [an anagram of Chopin] played "The Little Jew" '. The tentative suggestion was first put forward by Marceli Antoni Szulc (1873); it has been taken up by subsequent biographers as if it were an established fact.

Szafarnia was part of the estate of the friend of the Chopin family, Dominik Dziewanowski.

For the final version, see 77.

MS. Lost.

9

VARIATIONS in E major for Flute and Pianoforte on a theme by Rossini (from *La Cenerentola*?). 1824.

Publication:

    A facsimile reproduction in *Chopin in der Heimat*, Cracow, 1955, p. 269.

The theme is no. 12 of the opera, sung by Cenerentola to the words 'Non più mesta...'. The first performance of *La Cenerentola* in Warsaw was not until 29 August 1829. Since the same theme also occurs in Rossini's *Il Barbiere di Siviglia*, first performed in Warsaw in 1825, the variations may have been inspired by that opera and not the other. The manuscript gives neither source for the theme. The Variations are said to have been written by Chopin for Josef Cichocki, a famous flute-player in Warsaw. The manuscript was formerly in the possession of Josef Nowakowski. The work is not accepted by all authorities as authentic. MS. Society of Music, Warsaw.

10

RONDO in C minor, Op. 1. May 1825.

Publication:

Andrea Brzezina, Warsaw, June 1825.
Republished by:

(*a*) A. M. Schlesinger, Berlin (2019), December 1835.
(*b*) M. Schlesinger, Paris (1986), January 1836.
(*c*) Wessel, London (1423), March 1836.
(*d*) Hofmeister, Leipzig (2375), 1838.

Dedicated to Mme Linde, wife of Dr Samuel Bogumił Linde, philologist, friend and colleague of Nicolas Chopin, and Rector of the Warsaw Conservatoire.

It was announced in the Warsaw *Kuryer*, 2 June 1825, by Brzezina, and published by him without opus number (also without publisher's number). It was called 'Op. 1' on republication in Berlin. Brzezina's firm was taken over by Gustav Sennewald, Warsaw, *c*. 1830. On 27 November 1831 Louise Chopin wrote to her brother: 'Hofmeister has written to Sennewald to send him all your works, those already printed and those to be printed.'

It is probable that this Rondeau was composed by Chopin in two versions, for PF. Solo and PF. Duet. An edition entitled 'Rondeau à quatre mains pour le pianoforte composé par Frédéric Chopin, Œuvre 1' was published by Hofmeister, Leipzig, early in 1834 (PN 1977), that is, four years before he published the version for PF. Solo. The title-page of the solo version bears the words: 'Ce Rondeau est arrangé aussi pour PFTE à 4 mains', but there is no suggestion that the arranger was other than Chopin himself.

Wessel entitled his edition *Adieu à Varsovie*. It formed no. 1 of his series 'L'Amateur Pianiste'.

The work has been erroneously called 'Rondeau on *Don Giovanni*' through confusion with the composer's Op. 2.

MS. Lost.

Lost work of 1825:

In November Chopin wrote to Białobłocki: 'I have done a new Polonaise on the "Barber" [Rossini's *Barber of Seville*] which is fairly well liked; I think of sending it to be lithographed tomorrow.' (For Białobłocki, see **1**.)

11

POLONAISE in D minor, Op. 71 (Posth.): no. 1. (?) 1825.

Publication:

    A. M. Schlesinger, Berlin (4397), May 1855.
    J. Meissonnier Fils, Paris (3528), July 1855.

Composed for Count Michał Skarbek. Chopin sent a copy of this Polonaise to Titus Woyciechowski in 1827, but the work was not dedicated to him.

Meissonnier's editions of the posthumous works were published without opus numbers. They were simply called *Livraisons I–VII*.

A facsimile of a fragmentary manuscript of the work was given in the *Illustrowany Kuryer Codzienny*, Cracow, 24 September 1934 (see **17**).

MS. Unknown. There are no tempo or expression marks on the manuscript. Arthur Hedley, the former owner, was of the opinion that the MS. might be in the hand of the composer's father, Nicolas, and that the work may be as early as 1820.

12

THREE ÉCOSSAISES, Op. 72 (Posth.): no. 3. 1826.

No. 1 in D major.
No. 2 in G major.
No. 3 in D flat major.

For publication of Op. 72, see **19**.

Several écossaises were composed at this period; only these have survived. See note after **17**.

MSS. Nos. 2 and 3, written on p. 2 of the song 'Piosnka Litewska' ('Lithuanian Song'): Memorial Library of Music, Stanford University, California. Copy in another hand.

Lost works of 1826:

    (*a*) Variations in F major for PF. Duet.

    (*b*) Waltz in C major.

The two works are listed by Louise Chopin, but the manuscripts were evidently lost before they could be published.

The Variations in F major were composed for Titus Woyciechowski (1810–89), the most intimate of Chopin's friends, a friendship dating from boyhood. Woyciechowski's estate was at Poturżyn.

12(A)

INTRODUCTION, THEME AND VARIATIONS,. CODA in D major, for Pianoforte Duet. 1826.

[PRIMO]

Publication:

    Polskie Wydawnictwo Muzycne (5835), Cracow, 1965, edited by Jan Ekier (see note).

The work was listed by Louise Chopin as 'Variations on an Irish National Air (from Thomas Moore) for PF. Duet', dated 1826, and given as 'in D major or B minor, 6/8'. The word 'Irish' has confused the issue. The air is taken from 'A Selection of Popular National Airs with symphonies and accompaniments by Sir John Stevenson, Mus. Doc. The words by Thomas Moore', J. Power, London, 23 April 1818. This volume was not called no. 1, although subsequent volumes were numbered 2 to 6. The melody is subtitled 'Venetian Air', in F major, 6/8, to the words

> O come to me when daylight sets,
> Sweet, then come to me . . .

It is a derivation of the well-known 'Carnaval de Venise', which Chopin later used as the basis for variations in the *Souvenir de Paganini* of 1829 (37).

The work was identified from the manuscripts copy by Władysław Hordyński, and his account of the manuscript, with a facsimile of the first extant page, appeared in the *Ruch Muzycny*, no. 15, August 1964.

There are five variations on the theme.

MS.   Incomplete, and a copy in another hand: Jagiellonian Library, Cracow.

The outer cover is missing. This folio contained the Secondo part of the Introduction and Thema (first page) and the end of the Primo part (last page). The music for these two missing pages was reconstructed by the editor for publication.

13

POLONAISE in B flat minor. July 1826.

Publication:

The Polonaise had been lithographed for Chopin in

Warsaw in 1826. It was republished as a supplement to the *Echo Muzyczne*, Warsaw, no. 12, 3 June 1881.
Breitkopf & Haertel, Leipzig: *Gesamtausgabe* of Chopin's works, vol. XIII, no. 16 (C.XIII. 2), December 1879.

The work was composed for Wilhelm Kolberg (7) on the occasion of Chopin's departure with his sister Emilia for the spa Reinertz. He and Kolberg had recently visited the National Theatre, Warsaw, to see Rossini's *La Gazza Ladra*. Chopin has headed his original sketch: 'Polonaise, F. F. Chopin' and above the Trio he has written: 'Au revoir!' Another hand (probably Kolberg's or his brother's) has added to the title: 'Adieu à Guil. Kolberg (en partant pour Reinertz) 1826', and to the Trio: 'Trio tiré d'un air de la Gazza Ladra par Rossini.' At the foot of the Trio these words, partly cancelled, have been added in the same hand: 'Quelques jours avant son départ, Ch. accompagné de Kolberg [...?] une représentation de la Gazza Ladra de Rossini. . . .'

The air, a short Cavatina, was a favourite of Kolberg's. It is 'Vieni fra queste braccia' ('Come to these arms'), Act 1, no. 4, and is sung by Giannetto (tenor) to the maid Ninetta. Rossini's aria is maestoso, in D major.[1] It was published by Diabelli, Vienna, in the series 'Philomele', no. 10 (PN 177), *c.* 1817. *La Gazza Ladra* was first performed at La Scala, Milan, 31 May 1817.

MS. Copy in another hand: Paris Conservatoire. It contains a substantial sketch for a 'Mazur-Oberski' in C major.

[1] See *Musical Times*, London, August 1954.

14

INTRODUCTION AND VARIATIONS in E major, on a German National Air ['Der Schweizerbub']. Summer 1826.

Publication:

> Karl (Tobias) Haslinger, Vienna (T.H. 8148), May 1851.
> Simon Richault, Paris (10,869), May 1851.
> Cocks, London (9728), January 1852.

Dedicated to Katarzyna Sowińska, *née* Schroeder, wife of General Josef Sowiński. Chopin is said to have written these variations for Mme Sowińska at her request, after she had heard the air sung by Henrietta Sontag, but she could not, in fact, have heard this singer until 1830 at the earliest. Louise mentioned in her letter to Chopin of 27 November 1831: 'Mme Sowińska always enquires after you with the greatest affection.'

The folk-song is Austrian, probably Tyrolean (see *Deutscher Liederhort*, L. Erk and F. M. Boehme, vol. III). Moscheles is said to have taken down and arranged the traditional airs of a group of Tyrolean singers who visited London in 1827: one of these airs was 'Der Schweizerbub'. Particulars are given in *Grove's Dictionary*, vol. III, under 'Moscheles'. The first verse runs:

> Steh nur auf, steh nur auf du junger Schweizerbua,
> Steh nur auf, es ist jetzt Zeit!
> Steh nur in Gottes Namen auf.
> Deine Kuha die sind schon auf der Alma drauf.
> Steh nur auf, du junger Schweizerbua!

The title means 'The Cattle-Boy' and would seem to be mistranslated if rendered 'The Swiss Boy'.

The Introduction is followed by five variations. Chopin's direction *semplice – senza ornamenti* reveals the contemporary practice of embellishment in performance.

Chopin deposited the manuscript with Tobias Haslinger in Vienna during his visit to the capital in August 1829. The publisher's number shows that publication was contemplated in 1840 (see also **23**).

Cocks's edition was no. 14 of a series called 'The Classical Pianist: a Selection of Movements from the Works of the Great Masters' edited by Brinley Richards.

MS. Library of the Polish Academy of Science, Cracow. It is inscribed by Oskar Kolberg: 'I received the manuscript from the wife of General Sowiński in 1852, and presented it to the Cracow Library on 19 June 1874.' This copy is not an autograph of Chopin's.

15

RONDO à la Mazur, in F major, Op. 5. 1826.

Publication:

Andrea Brzezina, Warsaw, 28 February 1828.

Republished by:

(*a*) Hofmeister, Leipzig (2121), May 1836.

(*b*) Schonenberger, Paris (608), May 1836.

(*c*) Wessel, London (1552), October 1837.

Dedicated to Mlle la Comtesse Alexandrina de Moriolles, daughter of Count de Moriolles and a pupil of Chopin's.

Her father was tutor to the son of the Grand Duke Constantine.

The work was published without opus number by Brzezina. It was called 'Op. 5' by Hofmeister, and Chopin had obviously reserved this number for the Rondo: by 1836 his other opus numbers had reached 27.

For Brzezina and Hofmeister, see **10**.

Wessel's edition, also without opus number, was called *Rondo à la Majourka*; later this was changed to *La Posiana: Rondo on a Mazur in F*. Wessel claimed that it was 'Edited by his pupil I. [*sic*] Fontana'. He reissued the Rondo *c.* 1846 as no. 11 of the series called 'Le Pianiste Moderne', advertised as a continuation of the series 'L'Amateur Pianiste'. His publisher's number suggests that publication was delayed.

MS. Lost.

16

TWO MAZURKAS. 1826.

    No. 1 in G major.
    No. 2 in B flat major.

    Each mazurka exists in two versions.

Publication:

First versions:
M. Leitgeber, Poznań, as no. 2 and no. 3 of three
mazurkas (M.L. 18), 5 January 1875.
Republished by Breitkopf & Haertel, Leipzig, in the
Chopin *Gesamtausgabe*, vol. XIII, 17 December 1879.

Second versions:
Warsaw, 1826. Each in a small, oblong format, without
title or publisher's name.
Republished by R. Friedlein, Warsaw (R. 25 F), May
1851.

The history of the publication of the two versions of
these two mazurkas is complex and obscure. The above facts
present the most likely explanation. Both versions of each
mazurka are published in the 'Mazurkas' volume of the
Polish 'Complete Edition' (vol. x), but the account of their
publication, given in the appendix of the volume, is unsatisfactory, principally because the date of Friedlein's publication seems to have been unknown to the editors, and also
because various reprints of the above editions in the Warsaw
Echo Muzyczne and elsewhere seem to be treated as original
sources.

Both mazurkas, together with the one in D major (below),
were said to be improvised by Chopin during dancing
entertainments at the home of Dr Samuel Linde, the Rector
of the Warsaw Lyceum (*c.* 1826), and written down by
friends of the composer. The Mazurka in G major was
known to them as the 'Kulawy' Mazurka because of the
style of the dance ('Kulawy' = lame).

Chopin left the first versions of the two mazurkas, in
manuscript, with his friend Wilhelm Kolberg, from whose
brother, Oskar, resident in Cracow, they passed eventually
to M. A. Szulc, who edited them for Leitgeber. The composer's second versions were lithographed in Warsaw, with
his permission, in 1826, and he is supposed to have revised
a copy of this printing in his own hand. This revised copy

was Friedlein's source; it went into the possession of Alexander Polinski (see **3**) and is now in the National Library, Warsaw.

Leitgeber's publication, with a foreword by Szulc, also included the Mazurka in D major (**31**) as no. 1 and the 'Lento con gran espressione' (**49**). Brahms, on his copy of this publication, wrote the words: 'Vol. XIII, no. 1, comp. 1825' and 'Vol. XIII, no. 2, comp. 1825' above the mazurkas respectively. This indicated their future positions in the Breitkopf & Haertel *Gesamtausgabe*.

The first mazurka, in G major, may have been performed by Chopin in August 1826, while he was at Reinertz.

In his letter to Jan Białobłocki of 8 January 1827, Chopin wrote of these two dances: 'They are already published; meanwhile I am leaving my Rondo à la Mazur, that I wanted to have lithographed, stifling among my papers, though it is earlier and therefore has more right to travel.'

MSS. Lost.

17

CONTREDANSE in G flat major. (?) 1827.

Publication:

A facsimile reproduction in the *Illustrowany Kuryer Codzienny* ('Illustrated Daily Courier'): Literary and Scientific Supplement, Cracow, 24 September 1934.

The Dance, twenty-seven bars long, was composed for Titus Woyciechowski (see note after **12**). The further information, that it was written for his name-day (4 January)

or for his birthday (4 March) in 1829, arises from the fact
that, associated with the manuscript, another music page
was found; it bore those dates and Chopin's signature. But
the pieces of music paper are quite unalike, and since the
dates and signature are written below the heading 'Introduction & Variations pour le Pianoforte', the second paper
evidently belongs to Op. 2 (**22**) and not to the Contredanse
at all.

The facsimile was reproduced also in *Szlakiem Chopina* by
Maria Mirska, Warsaw, 1935. The Dance, edited by Michael
Idzikowski, was printed in Warsaw in 1943.

MS.   This was preserved by the descendants of Woycie-
       chowski, but destroyed in the Second World War.

Lost works of 1827:

(*a*) Écossaise in B flat major.

(*b*) *Andante dolente* in B flat minor.

Both works are mentioned in the list of unpublished
works compiled by Louise Chopin. *Dolente* = doleful.

18

MAZURKA in A minor, Op. 68 (Posth.): no. 2. 1827.

Publication of Op. 68:

A. M. Schlesinger, Berlin (4394), May 1855.

J. Meissonnier Fils, Paris (3525), July 1855.

Meissonnier's editions of the posthumous works were
published without opus numbers.

MS. Lost.

19

NOCTURNE in E minor, Op. 72 (Posth.): no. 1. 1827.

Publication of Op. 72:

> A. M. Schlesinger, Berlin (4400), May 1855.
> J. Meissonnier Fils, Paris (3531), July 1855.

Meissonnier's editions of the posthumous works were published without opus numbers.

MS. Lost.

20

FUNERAL MARCH in C minor, Op. 72 (Posth.): no. 2. 1827.

Publication:

Version (*a*): A. M. Schlesinger, Berlin (4400), May 1855.
               J. Meissonnier Fils, Paris (3531), July 1855.
Version (*b*): Oxford Edition of *Chopin's Works*, vol. III, edited by E. Ganche, London, 1932.

The date is according to Louise's list; Fontana gives 1829.

Meissonnier's editions of the posthumous works were published without opus numbers.

MSS. 1. Version (*a*): Lost.
      2. Version (*b*): A copy of this version, made by Tellefsen in May 1850 for Marcellina Czartoryska (formerly with Arthur Hedley): Unknown.

21

WALTZ in A flat major. 1827.

Publication:

Breitkopf & Haertel, Leipzig, in a supplement to the *Gesamtausgabe* of Chopin's works ('Klavierbibliothek', 23, 183 : 11), 1902.
F. Hoesick, Warsaw, 1902.

The Waltz was discovered in an album which had belonged to Emily Elsner, the daughter of Josef Elsner (see **23**). Her album also contained a Waltz in E flat (**46**), the first version of the Mazurka in A minor, Op. 7: no. 2 (**45**), and seven of the songs of Op. 74 (see Appendix VIII for details). Breitkopf & Haertel, in their supplement, published the three instrumental pieces.

There was another copy of this waltz originally among the Chopin family papers.

MSS. (1) Lost.
      (2) Emily Elsner's album (partially destroyed): Society of Music, Warsaw.

22

VARIATIONS in B flat major on a theme from Mozart's
Don Giovanni ('Là ci darem la mano'), for PF. and Orchestra,
Op. 2. Strzyżewo, late summer 1827.

Publication:

> Tobias Haslinger, Vienna (5489), January 1830.
> M. Schlesinger, Paris (1312), Early 1833.
> Wessel, London (820), Spring 1833.

Dedicated to Titus Woyciechowski (see note after **12** and
17).

The theme comes from the duet sung by Don Giovanni
and Zerlina in Act 1, no. 7. Schumann's article containing
the words 'Hats off, gentlemen, a genius!' deals with this
work of Chopin's.

Strzyżewo is a country place some 150 miles to the south-
west of Warsaw.

The work was first performed by the composer on 11
August 1829 in the Kärntnertortheater, Vienna. The
performance in Warsaw followed on 8 July 1830 at a
concert given by the singer Mme Meyer.

The Variations were published as 'Lieferung 27' in
Haslinger's serial publication *Odéon*, described as 'Aus-

gewählte grosse Concert-Stücke für verschiedene Instru-
mente' ('Selected Grand Concert Pieces for various
instruments'); it was the first of Chopin's compositions to be
published outside Poland. The manuscript was in Haslinger's
hands by the summer of 1828, sent to him by Josef Elsner
(see next). In 1839 Haslinger published an arrangement for
PF. Solo (T.H. 7714).

Wessel's edition is entitled *Homage* [*sic*] *à Mozart* and forms
book XVII of the 'Album des Pianistes de Première Force';
this is described as 'A Collection of the most Brilliant and
Original Compositions' and contained pieces by Hummel,
Czerny, Pixis, among others. The English edition was
dedicated without authorisation to Charles Czerny.

The French edition was based on a printed copy of the
Viennese edition, corrected by Chopin himself.

The manuscript in the Vienna Nationalbibliothek (see
below) contains a cancelled variation, the fourth, and in its
place Chopin has brought forward the original no. 6.[1] The
work thus contained in its first form *seven* variations, the
last serving as a finale. The cancelled variation is reproduced
in Franz Zagiba's *Chopin und Wien*, Vienna, 1951, p. 24.

MSS. (1) Original manuscript, with drawings and com-
ments in Chopin's hand, 66 pages: Robert O.
Lehmann Foundation, Washington.[2]
(2) Nationalbibliothek, Vienna.
(3) Two pages, containing the beginning of Var. V:
Maison Pleyel, Paris.

Lost work of 1828:

Waltz in D minor. The work is given in Louise's list, with
the date and entitled (? by Louise) 'La Partenza' ('The
Departure').

[1] See *Musical Times*, London, August 1954.
[2] See *Chopin* (rev. ed.), Arthur Hedley, London, 1963 pp. 16–17.

23

SONATA in C minor, Op. 4 (Posth.). Early 1828.

Publication:

Karl Haslinger, Vienna (T.H. 8147), May 1851.
Simon Richault, Paris (10,868), May 1851.
Cocks, London (9727), January 1852.

Dedicated to Josef Elsner (1769–1854), Silesian composer and first principal of the Warsaw Conservatoire, Chopin's tutor in composition. It was he who sent the MS. of the Sonata to Haslinger in the summer of 1828. Chopin wrote: 'As a pupil of Elsner's I dedicated [the Sonata] to him.' Elsner's acceptance of the dedication is written on the autograph in his own hand. The inscription on MS. reads:

Sonata pour le pianoforte dediée à Mr Josef Elsner, Professeur à l'Université Royale de Varsovie, Membre de la Société Philomatique de Varsovie, Chevalier de l'order de St Stanislas etc., etc., Composée par Frédéric Chopin. Œuvre 3 [*sic*].

The real Op. 3 (**41**) had appeared in 1831–3, and so the opus number of the Sonata was altered to 4. Karl Haslinger published the work without the dedication to Elsner. His father and predecessor in the business, Tobias Haslinger, had engraved the Sonata as early as the summer of 1839, which accounts for the publisher's number. Chopin refused to correct the proofs. But Haslinger must have passed these proofs privately to musicians in Germany and Austria, for during August 1839 Chopin wrote to Julian Fontana: 'My father writes that my old Sonata has been published by Haslinger and that the Germans praise it.' Several years later he wrote to his family on 1 October 1845: 'The Sonata dedicated to Elsner has been published in Vienna by Haslinger.'

The London publication was referred to by Jane Stirling in her letter to Louise Chopin of January 1852. It is no. 13 of a series called 'The Classical Pianist' (see **14**).

MS. Robert O. Lehmann Foundation, Washington (formerly part of the Louis Kock Collection, with Rudolf Floersheim, Muzzano-Lugano, Switzerland). The MS. is dated '1828'.

24

POLONAISE in B flat major, Op. 71 (Posth.): no. 2. 1828.

Publication:

A. M. Schlesinger, Berlin (4398), May 1855.
J. Meissonnier Fils, Paris (3529), July 1855.

Meissonnier's editions of the posthumous works were published without opus numbers.

MS. Unknown. (There are no tempo or expression marks of any kind. It contains the first few bars of the Polonaise in F minor (**30**).) The manuscript may be a copy by Louise Chopin.

25

TRIO in G minor, for PF., vn. and cello, Op. 8. Poznań, mid-1828 – Warsaw, early 1829.

Publication:

  F. Kistner, Leipzig (999), December 1832.
  M. Schlesinger, Paris (1344), November 1833.
  Wessel, London (924), July 1833.

Dedicated to Prince Antoine Radziwill (1775–1833),

German-Polish cellist and composer, Governor of the Grand
Duchy of Poznań. He accepted the dedication in a warm
letter of thanks to Chopin dated 4 November 1829.

The work was published in Leipzig as *Premier Trio*. The
first movement, *allegro*, was finished by early September
1828 and the composer in a letter of 27 December 1828 to
Woyciechowski referred to the whole work as 'not quite
finished'. In a letter to the same friend on 31 August 1830,
Chopin wondered whether to rewrite the work with viola
instead of violin.

Schlesinger's edition was a republication in Paris of what
had hitherto been an exclusive German publication. At that
date he also brought out the mazurkas, Opp. 6 and 7 (**60 and
61**), which had previously been published only by Kistner
in Leipzig.

Op. 8 was often missing in Wessel's advertised lists of
the English edition of the composer's works. He published
an arrangement of the work by T. Clinton for Flute, cello
and PF. (PN 930). In September 1838 he issued it as no. 1 of
a series of 'Modern Trios for PF., vn. & cello'. Occasionally
Wessel (e.g. in 1841) advertised the first two nocturnes of
Op. 9 as 'Op. 8', calling the third nocturne 'Op. 9'.

MSS. (1) Sketches for the Trio, including others for the
PF. Concerto, Op. 21.

(2) Fair copy of the score.
Both MSS. in the Chopin Institute, Warsaw.

26

RONDO in C major, for PF. Solo (orginal version of Op. 73).
Sanniki, summer 1828.

Publication:

>Vol. XII of the Dzieła Wszystkie ('Complete Works')
>of Chopin, Warsaw, 1954.

A facsimile of part of the autograph was reproduced in
Chopin und Wien, Zagiba, Vienna, 1951, p. 112. A facsimile
of the whole autograph (four pages) is given in the Warsaw
edition.

The autograph manuscript contains in Chopin's hand:
'à M. Fuchs, F. F. Chopin', and in Fuchs's hand: 'Received
from the composer himself, as a gift, and bequeathed to the
Musikverein here by Alois Fuchs, Vienna, November 1840.'
Chopin gave Fuchs the manuscript in June 1831.

Sanniki is a small country district some fifty miles south-
west of Warsaw. It belonged to a family named Pruszak,
friends of the composer.

MS. Archives of the Gesellschaft der Musikfreunde, Vienna
(the Musikverein).

27

RONDO in C major, for two Pianofortes (final version), Op.
73 (Posth.). Sanniki, August 1828.

Publication:

>A. M. Schlesinger, Berlin (4401), May 1855.
>J. Meissonnier Fils, Paris (3532), July 1855.

Meissonnier's editions of the posthumous works were
published without opus numbers. Schlesinger also published

arrangements for PF. Duet (Op. 73 A) and for PF. Solo (Op. 73 B).

The work is an arrangement of the previous item by Chopin. In a letter to Woyciechowski of 9 September 1828 he wrote: 'Today I tried it with Ernemann at Buchholtz's [a PF. manufacturer] and it came out pretty well. We think of playing it some day at the Ressource.' Later, on 27 December 1828, in another letter to the same friend, he referred to it as 'that orphan child' which had found a stepfather in Julian Fontana (see 120).

The Ressource was a private association of musical amateurs in Warsaw. For Sanniki, see previous item.

MS. Lost.

28

GRAND FANTASIA in A major, on Polish Airs, for PF. and Orchestra, Op. 13. November 1828.

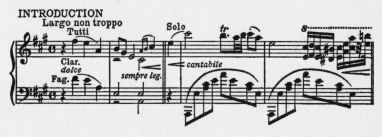

Publication:

    Kistner, Leipzig (1033–4), May 1834.

    M. Schlesinger, Paris (1574), April 1834.

    Wessel, London (1083), April 1834.

(This is the first work of Chopin's to be published simultaneously in Germany, France and England. The practice persisted for the next thirteen years until the publication of Op. 64.) The Leipzig publication was announced in the *A.M.Z.* for December 1833.

Dedicated to Johann Peter Pixis (1788–1874), German pianist and composer, resident in Paris from 1825 to 1845.

Among the Polish airs used are these:

(1) The folk-song 'Już miesiąc zaszedł, psy się uśpiły' ('Already the moon had set, the dogs were asleep').

(2) An air by Karol (Kasimir) Kurpiński.

(3) A *Kujawiak*, which is a dance of the Kujawia district, called by Chopin a 'Mazovian' air. ('The *Kujawiak* is a species of Mazurka – according to all the authorities the slowest kind of Mazurka, though Chopin marks his *vivace*': Gerald Abraham, *Chopin's Musical Style*, London, 1939, p. 23.)

Breitkopf & Haertel announced publication of Chopin's Op. 13 (which they called '3 Nocturnes') *recte* Op. 15 – in *A.M.Z.* for November 1833. In December 1833 Kistner advertised the forthcoming publication of Opp. 13 and 14, correctly entitled, with the comment – "ebenfalls mit Eigenthums-Recht"!

Kistner issued the Fantasia in two versions, with and without orchestral accompaniment.

Wessel published the work as book XXI of the 'Album des Pianistes de Première Force' (see **22**), and claimed that it, as well as Opp. 14, 21 and 22, were expressly composed for the series.

The first performance of the Fantasia took place on 3 March 1830 in the National Theatre, Warsaw, with the composer as soloist.

Kurpiński (1785–1857), Polish violinist and composer, was a professor at the Warsaw Conservatoire.

MS. First sketch, fragment. Bars 1–19 of the Introduction, bars 34 and 35 (PF. part only) of the Fantasia, with sketches for the instrumental parts: Dr Martin Bodmer, Coligny, Geneva, Switzerland.

29

KRAKOWIAK: Grand Concert Rondo in F major, for PF. and Orchestra, Op. 14. November–December 1828.

Publication:

Kistner, Leipzig (1038–9), July 1834.
M. Schlesinger, Paris (1586), June 1834.
Wessel, London (1084), May 1834.

Kistner's publication was announced in *A.M.Z.* in December 1833.

Dedicated to Mme la Princesse Adam Czartoryska (Marcellina, *née* Radziwill), exiled Polish princess, pupil and lifelong friend of Chopin.

In a letter of 27 December 1828 to Woyciechowski, the composer wrote: 'The score of the *Rondo à la Krakowiak* is finished.'

A Krakowiak is a Polish dance in 2/4 time of the Cracow district.

Kistner issued the work with and without orchestral accompaniment. This was Chopin's last publication in Leipzig from Kistner: after this his work was published exclusively in Germany from Breitkopf & Haertel.

Wessel published the work as book XXII of his 'Album des Pianistes de Première Force' (see 22 and previous item).

Schlesinger simultaneously published arrangements of the orchestral part for (*a*) string quartet and (*b*) a second pianoforte.

MS. Czartoryski Library, National Museum, Cracow. The manuscript is now bound in green plush, with the Bovy medallion portrait of Chopin stamped on the cover in gilt. It was presented by Chopin, with an autograph dedication, to his friend Adolf Cichowski (1794–1854). The composer added: 'published in 1831 or 1832', which is, of course, an imperfect memory.

30

POLONAISE in F minor, Op. 71 (Posth.): no. 3. 1828.

Publication:

    A. M. Schlesinger, Berlin (4399), May 1855.
    J. Meissonnier Fils, Paris (3530), July 1855.

Meissonnier's editions of the posthumous works were published without opus numbers.

The date is according to Louise's list: Fontana gives 1829.

The work was played and greatly liked by Princess Radziwill during Chopin's visit to Antonin in October 1829.

MSS. (1) Sketch of the first few bars, dated 1829 (see **24**): Unknown.

    (2) First draft, complete in essentials: David Opochinsky, New York.

    (3) Fair copy, dated 'Stuttgart, 1836': National Library, Warsaw.

31

MAZURKA in D major (first version). 1829.

Publication:

M. Leitgeber, Poznan (M.L. 18), 5 January 1875.

Leitgeber's edition, edited and with a foreword by M. A. Szulc, included the Mazurkas in G major and B flat major (**16**) and the 'Lento con gran espressione' (**49**).

The work was revised considerably in 1832 (see **71**).

Brahms wrote on his copy: 'Bd. XIII: no. 6. comp. 1829.' This indicated its future position in the Breitkopf & Haertel *Gesamtausgabe* (see **16**).

MS. Lost.

32

SONG for voice and PF., Op. 74: no. 5. 1829.
   'Gdzie lubi' ('Strumyk lubi w dolinie')
   'There where she loves' ('A stream loves the vale').
                    (A major)
German title: 'Was ein junges Mädchen liebt.'
Text: Stefan Witwicki.

Publication of Op. 74:

A. M. Schlesinger, Berlin:

(*a*)   A Polish edition entitled *Zbiór Speiwów Polskich* ('A Collection of Polish Songs') (4638–53), 1857.

(*b*)   A German edition, with translations by Ferdinand Gumbert [no Polish text interlined] (4797–4812), Op. 74: nos. 1–4, December 1859; Op. 74: nos. 5–16, January 1860.

Gebethner & Wolff, Warsaw (84–99), 1859.

Op. 74 contained originally only sixteen songs. No. 17, 'Śpiew Grobowy' ('Hymn from the Tomb'), was added later, *c*. 1868 (see **101**).

The complete seventeen songs of Op. 74 were issued later by:

1. A. M. Schlesinger, Berlin, in two versions: for Soprano or Tenor (6669) and for Alto or Bass (6670), 1874.
2. Karl Haslinger, Vienna, *c*. 1870.
3. Breitkopf & Haertel, Leipzig, with new translations by Hans Schmidt, *c*. 1874.
4. Stanley Lucas, Weber & Co., London (299), with English translations by the Rev. J. J. Troutbeck, from the German text of Gumbert, 1874.
5. J. Hamelle, Paris (1467). June 1879.
6. Gebethner & Wolff, Warsaw. 1880.

Peter's Edition of the songs, *c*. 1887, with translations by Wilhelm Henzen and Max Kalkbeck, still contained only the original sixteen songs.

Two of the songs from Op. 74 – no. 10, 'Wojak' ('The Warrior') and no. 1, 'Zycenie' ('The Wish') (see **47** and **33**) – had already been published as '2 Spiewy' ('2 Songs') by the firm A. Kocipiński, Kiev (44 and 48), in 1856. These were reissues of an anonymous publication by the same firm in 1837.[1]

---

[1] See the *Musical Quarterly*, New York, January 1856.

Gebethner used Schlesinger's plates for the edition of 1859, which was reviewed by Josef Sowiński in the *Revue Musicale*, Warsaw, no. 40, 1859.

Wessel had refused the songs in 1854 as unsaleable in England, although he was referring to a *Polish text* edition.

The songs of Op. 74, together with two further songs not included there (**51** and **132**), are published in the Polish 'Complete Edition', vol. XVII, 1951.

In the announcement of a concert given in Paris on 14 January 1856, Fontana referred to the six Polish songs in the programme as still unpublished. This disposes of the date usually given (1855) for the publication of Op. 74. Fontana contributed a foreword to Schlesinger's editions of the songs.

The poems by Witwicki which Chopin set to music were all published in his *Piosnki Sielskie* ('Pastoral Songs'), Warsaw, 1830. The composer, however, knew them in manuscript (see **51**).

MSS. (1) Emily Elsner's album (partially destroyed): Society of Music, Warsaw.

    (2) Copy by Louise in Maria Wodzińska's album: State Collection, Warsaw.

There is a complete manuscript transcript of the songs, used by Schlesinger for the 1859 publication, and made by Fontana and another (? Franchomme) in the possession of Antony van Hoboken, Ascona, Switzerland.

33

SONG for voice and PF., Op. 74: no. 1. 1829.
    'Życzenie' ('Gdybym ja była słoneczkiem na niebie')
    'The Wish' ('Were I the sun in the sky').
          (G major)

German title: 'Mädchens Wunsch'.
Text: Stefan Witwicki.

Publication:

Anton Kocipiński, Kiev (48), *c.* 1856. This was possibly
a republication of an anonymous edition of the song by
this firm from 1837.

For details of its publication in Op. 74, see **32**.

Fontana transposed the song into A major for the Op. 74
edition, and made several alterations in the musical text.
Chopin's version of the opening is given here under (*a*),
Fontana's alteration under (*b*).

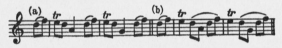

Liszt used the song in his *Glanes de Woronince*; no. 2 is
called 'Mélodies Polonaises' and 'Życzenie' is the second of
these melodies *allegretto amoroso*. He was under the impression
that it was a folk-song, and thus he may have used the
Kocipiński copy of the 1837 edition mentioned above.
Glanes de Woronince was published by Kistner, Leipzig, in
1849.

Liszt also transcribed the song for PF. Solo (*6 Chants
Polonais*: no. 1) published by A. M. Schlesinger, 1860.

'Życzenie' was transposed into B flat major and furnished
with words by George Sand. Her poem begins:

Quand la lune se lève / Dans un pale rayon,
Elle vient comme un rêve, / Comme une vision.

This version was published as 'La Reine des Songes' in the
Journal de Musique, Paris, no. 8, 22 July 1876. The *Journal*
published several musical supplements by Chopin in 1876–7;

the July issue was devoted to George Sand and Chopin. It contained as supplement these three pieces:

(*a*) 'La Reine des Songes';
(*b*) *Rondo* (extracted from Op. 11);
(*c*) 74 bars in A minor, from the 'Bolero', Op. 19, entitled 'Chanson de Zingara: souvenir du voyage en Espagne' (see **81**).

There were three autographs of this song. (1) A copy in the possession of the Chopin family was first reproduced in 1901 by Mieczysław Karlowicz in his book now generally known in its French version: *Souvenirs inédits de Chopin*, Paris, 1904. (2) A copy in Emily Elsner's album. (3) A copy by Louise Chopin in Maria Wodzińska's album (1836). See below.

MSS. (1) Leopold Binental's Collection: lost in the Second World War.
(2) Society of Music, Warsaw: similarly destroyed.
(3) State Collection, Warsaw.

34

MAZURKA in F major, Op. 68 (Posth.): no. 3. 1829.

Publication of Op. 68:

    A. M. Schlesinger, Berlin (4394), May 1855.
    J. Meissonnier Fils, Paris (3525), July 1855.

Meissonnier's editions of the posthumous works were published without opus numbers.

The section *poco più vivo* is from the folk-tune 'Oj Magdalino':

MS. Lost.

35

WALTZ in B minor, Op. 69 (Posth.): no. 2. 1829.

Publication:

> J. Wildt, Cracow (no publisher's number), 1852.
> Wessel, London (8015), July 1853.

Republished as Op. 69: no. 2 by:

> A. M. Schlesinger, Berlin (4395), May 1855.
> J. Meissonnier Fils, Paris (3526), July 1855.

Meissonnier's editions of the posthumous works were published without opus numbers.

Wildt's publication, which also included the Waltz in F minor, Op. 70: no. 2 (**138**), was entitled:

> Une soirée en 1844. Deux valses mélancoliques
> écrites sur l'album de Mme la Comtesse Pxxx.

The Countess was probably Delphine Potocka (43) but the waltz in B minor was originally written for Wilhelm Kolberg (see 7).

Wessel's title was similar to that of the original publisher but with the characteristic addition: 'Une soirée à Cracovie en 1844 . . .'

The two waltzes were also published in England (April 1854) by J. J. Ewer, London.

Fontana was aware of the fact that these two waltzes had already been published when he included them in the posthumous opus numbers which he sponsored in 1855. This is clear from the letter which he received from Breitkopf & Haertel on 14 March 1854. His manuscript is lost.

MSS. (1) The copy in Delphine Potocka's album: unknown. It was formerly in the possession of Alexander Tyszkiewicz, Mohylow.

(2) Jagiellonian Library, Cracow University. This MS. is inscribed by Oskar Kolberg, the brother of Wilhelm, who presented it to Cracow University on 29 March 1881. This autograph was used as the basis of the waltz published in vol. 1 of the *Oxford Edition of Chopin's Works*, London, 1932.

(3) Conservatoire, Paris: unsigned and undated, together with 92.

36

POLONAISE in G flat major. 1829 (probably before July, when Chopin left Warsaw for Vienna).

Publication:

> J. Kauffmann, Warsaw (170), 1870.
> B. Schott's Sons, Mainz (20,029), 1870.

Republished by:

> (*a*) *Die Musik*, Berlin, October 1908.
> (*b*) Leon Chojecki, Warsaw, 1909.

Both these republications were erroneously believed to be first editions.

The Polonaise, fifty-eight bars long, with a Trio in E flat minor of seventy bars, is named in Louise's list, so that the MS. was extant in the 1850s. Niecks queried the authenticity of the work: 'Nothing but the composer's autograph would convince one of the genuineness of the piece.'

MS. Lost.

37

VARIATIONS in A major ('Souvenir de Paganini'). Summer 1829.

Publication:

> Supplement to *Echo Muzyczne*, Warsaw, no. 5, 1881.

The work is quite short, ninety-one bars. The manuscript was formerly in the possession of Chopin's friend, Josef Nowakowski, and from him it passed to the Warsaw composer and music teacher, Adam Minhejmer,[1] who secured its publication. Jan Kleczyński wrote a preface for this publication. The work was republished in vol. XIII of the

---

[1] Better known by the German form of his name, Münchenheimer. In 1892 he also owned the MSS. of **5, 9** and **28**.

Polish 'Complete Edition', 1954, and also as no. 3 of 'Classical Discoveries', edited by Jack Werner, Elkin & Co., London (2438), 1956.

The theme of these variations is the Venetian air 'Le Carnaval de Venise', used by Paganini himself as the basis of variations in his Op. 10. Ludwik Bronarski suggested that Paganini may have played this Op. 10 during his visit to Warsaw (23 May to 19 July 1829) and that Chopin heard his playing of it.

MS. Unknown. It was exhibited at the International Exhibition, Vienna, 1892.

38

MAZURKA in C major, Op. 68 (Posth.): no. 1. 1829.

Publication of Op. 68:

    A. M. Schlesinger, Berlin (4394), May 1855.

    J. Meissonnier Fils, Paris (3525), July 1855.

Meissonnier's editions of the posthumous works were published without opus numbers.

MS. Lost.

39

MAZURKA in G major. 22 August 1829

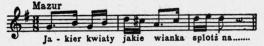

Publication:

    Dalibor, Prague, no. 6, 20 February 1879.

The piece was written in the album of Vaclav Hanka

(1791–1861), philologist and librarian, the curator of the Prague Museum. Chopin wrote to his family from Dresden on 26 August 1829: 'Luckily Maciejowski hit on the idea of writing a four-verse Mazurka, so I set it to music and inscribed myself together with my poet as originally as possible.'

Ignacy Maciejowski accompanied the composer on the return journey from Vienna to Warsaw. His poem celebrates Czech–Polish friendship and actually consists of five, not four, verses. It begins:

> Jakier kwiaty, jakie wianka
> Splotę na czesc Hanki . . .

Chopin's setting is twelve bars long, in G major and 3/8 time. It consists of the vocal line only.

Dalibor was a Czech periodical published three times a month from 1879 to 1913. The music of the Mazurka was contained in an article 'Chopin in Prague in 1829' by Dr Otkar Hostińsky (1847–1910), a distinguished Czech musicologist and Professor of Aesthetics at the Caroline University, Prague. His article also gave Maciejowski's poem, and the two letters from Chopin to his family of 19 and 26 August 1829.

MS. National Museum, Prague. When Hanka's album was rebound some years ago, the margins were so deeply cut that almost half Chopin's autograph was removed in the operation.

40

WALTZ in D flat major, Op. 70 (Posth.): no. 3. 3 October 1829.

*In some editions, ♭

Publication of Op. 70:

    A. M. Schlesinger, Berlin (4396), May 1855.

    J. Meissonnier Fils, Paris (3527), July 1855.

Meissonnier's editions of the posthumous works were published without opus numbers.

The Waltz was written for Konstancja Gładkowska (1810–1889), singer and friend of Chopin's youth.

The composer wrote to Titus Woyciechowski on 3 October 1829: '... [Konstancja] inspired me this morning to write the little waltz I am sending you.' He drew his friend's attention to bars 32–7: '... no one but you will know what they mean.' This reference has led to the identification of the Waltz.

Fontana's date is 1830.

MS. Lost.

40(B)

WALTZ in A minor (sketch). (?) 1829.

Unpublished

The manuscript consists of sketches for a brief prelude and the main theme.

MS. Unknown. Formerly in the possession of H. Hinterberger, Vienna.

41

POLONAISE in C major, for PF. and cello, Op. 3. Antonin, 20–28 October 1829.

Publication:

Pietro Mechetti, Vienna (2178), Autumn 1831.

Republished by:

(*a*) A. M. Schlesinger, Berlin, 1832.

(*b*) Simon Richault, Paris (3301), June 1835.

(*c*) Wessel, London (PF. 1662), (cello, 1663), April 1836.

Dedicated to Josef Merk (1795–1852), eminent Viennese cellist and professor at the Conservatoire.

The work was composed for Prince Antoine Radziwill (cello) and his daughter Wanda (piano) (see **25**). Antonin was the seat of Prince Antoine. Chopin, in a letter of 14 November to Woyciechowski, refers to the Polonaise as 'alla polacca'. He composed the Introduction later (see **52**).

Op. 3 was published by Mechetti earlier than 1833, the date usually given. This is shown by his publisher's number and also by the date of the Berlin republication. Mechetti published an arrangement for PF. Solo, made by Czerny, *c.* 1834, and early in 1836 he issued the work for PF. and cello *or* violin (2723). The firm of Mechetti was bought by C. A. Spina, also of Vienna, in 1855.

A. M. Schlesinger's arrangement for PF. Solo appeared in 1842.

The French edition was bought from Richault by M. Schlesinger, Paris, *c.* 1841; in 1842 Schlesinger published an arrangement for PF. Solo (3729).

Wessel's edition is entitled *La Gaîeté*. His arrangement for PF. Solo, published in October 1837 (publisher's number 1860), was republished *c.* 1845 as no. 50 in his series 'Le Pianiste Moderne'. In November 1838 he published an arrangement for PF. and viola, and in 1840 an arrangement for PF. and flute (arr. by J. Sedlatzek).

MS. Lost.

42

FOUR STUDIES from Op. 10. October–November 1829.

> No. 8 in F major.
> No. 9 in F minor.
> No. 10 in A flat major.
> No. 11 in E flat major.

Publication of Op. 10:

> Kistner, Leipzig (two parts: 1018–19), August 1833.
> M. Schlesinger, Paris (1399), 8 June 1833.
> Wessel, London (book I: 960; book II: 961), August
> 1833.

Dedicated to Liszt. The Paris edition carries the dedication as '... à son ami J. [*sic*] Liszt'.

Wessel's edition is dedicated to '... ses amis J. Liszt et Ferd. Hiller'. For a note on Wessel's edition, see **53**.

The copyright of Op. 10, together with that of the second set of Studies, Op. 25, was sold by Schlesinger at the end of 1844 to the Paris publisher Henri Lemoine.

These four studies were originally intended to be Op. 10: nos. 7–10, but were displaced by the Study in C major, the present Op. 10: no. 7.

One of these four studies was written before 20 October 1829, the others soon afterwards; we read in Chopin's letter to Woyciechowski of 20 October 1829: 'I have composed a big *Exercice en forme* in a way of my own; I will show it to you when we meet.' Later he wrote to the same friend, on 14 November 1829: 'I have written two studies; I could play them well to you.'

No. 11, in E flat major, is the 'Arpeggio' Study.

MSS. (1) Nos. 8, 9 and 10: State Collection, Warsaw (formerly in the Deutsche Staatsbibliothek, Berlin).

(2) No. 11: Rudolf Nydahl, Stockholm (Stiftelsen Musikkulturens främjande).

43

CONCERTO in F minor for PF. and Orchestra, Op. 21. Autumn 1829 to early 1830.

Publication:

> Breitkopf & Haertel, Leipzig (5654), April 1836.
> M. Schlesinger, Paris (1940), October 1836.
> Wessel, London (1642), November 1836.

Dedicated to Mme la Comtesse Delphine Potocka, *née* Komar, a gifted singer, pupil and close friend of the composer.

The Larghetto was finished by September 1829; the Finale followed late in 1829 or early 1830. According to a letter from Chopin to Woyciechowski of 3 October 1829, the slow movement was inspired by Konstancja Gładkowska (see **40**).

The work was called 'Second Concerto' on publication, although it is the first in order of composition. Delay in preparing the orchestral parts led to the publication of the later Concerto in E minor (**53**) before this one.

It was first performed privately in Chopin's home, with Kurpiński conducting, on 3 March 1830; the public performance in the National Theatre, Warsaw, followed a fortnight later.

Breitkopf & Haertel issued an arrangement for PF. Solo shortly after the first publication. They also published an arrangement of the orchestral part for String Quintet.

Wessel published the Concerto as book XXIII of his series 'Album des Pianistes de Première Force' (see **22**). It was dedicated without the composer's sanction, or knowledge, to 'Mrs Anderson' (Mrs Lucy Anderson, of Bath, 1790–1878), PF. teacher to Queen Victoria and her children.

The *Oxford Edition* of 1932, edited by Ganche, published for the first time a passage for the bass (left hand), written by Chopin for bars 43–70 of the Larghetto to be played when the movement is performed as a PF. Solo.

Karl Klindworth's arrangement was made in London in 1868 and published in 1878 by P. Jurgenson, Moscow, under the title: 'Second Concerto de Chopin, Op. 21, avec un nouvel accompagnement d'orchestre d'après la partition originale par K. Klindworth. Dédié à Fr. Liszt.' This publication became the property of Bote & Bock, Berlin.

MSS. (1) Sketches: see **25**.

    (2) Chopin Institute, Warsaw (formerly with Breit-
kopf & Haertel). The PF. part only in the
composer's hand.

44

WALTZ in E major. 1829.

Publication:

    W. Chaberski, Cracow (no publisher's number), 1871.
Republished by:

    Gebethner & Wolff, Warsaw (. . .), 1877.

    The date is given as 1830 in Louise's list. Its publication
by Chaberski is mentioned by Szulc in his book on Chopin
(1873).

MS. Lost.

45

MAZURKA in A minor, Op. 70 (Posth.): no. 2 (first version).
1829.

Publication:

    Breitkopf & Haertel, Leipzig, in a supplement to their *Gesamtausgabe* of Chopin's works ('Klavierbibliothek': 21, 183 III), 1902.

    F. Hoesick, Warsaw, 1902.

This version of the mazurka was written in Emily Elsner's album. It has a short introduction (8 bars) in A major, marked *Duda* (= bagpipe). There are other details which differ from the final version in Op. 7 (**61**); the chief of these is at bars 29–32, where the first version has:

MS. Emily Elsner's album (partially destroyed): Society of
    Music, Warsaw.

46

W A L T Z in E flat major. 1829–30.

Publication:

    Breitkopf & Haertel, Leipzig, in a supplement to their *Gesamtausgabe* of Chopin's works ('Klavierbibliothek': 23, 183 I), 1902.

The date for the Waltz is given in Louise's list. The publication took place after the discovery of a copy in Emily

Elsner's album (see **21**). Not all authorities accept the authenticity of this work.

MSS. (1) The copy in the Chopin family papers: lost.
    (2) Emily Elsner's album (partially destroyed): Society of Music, Warsaw (a facsimile is given in the Polish 'Complete Works').

47

SONG for voice and PF., Op. 74: no. 10. Spring 1830.
    'Wojak' ('Rży moj gniady')
    'The Warrior' ('My bay horse neighs').
(A flat major)
German title: 'Der Reiter vor der Schlacht'.
Text: Stefan Witwicki.

Publication:

    A. Kocipiński, Kiev (44), 1856. Probably a reissue of an anonymous edition from this firm in 1837.

For details of the publication of Op. 74, see **32**.

MSS. (1) Rough draft: private possession in the U.S.A.
    (2) Emily Elsner's album (partially destroyed): Society of Music, Warsaw.
    (3) Maria Wodzińska's album: State Collection, Warsaw.
    (4) Fair copy: Artur Rubinstein.

48

SONG for voice and PF., Op. 74: no. 6. Spring 1830.
'Precz z moich oczu!' ('Precz z moich oczu! posłucham odrazu!')
'Out of my sight' ('Out of my sight!').
F minor-A flat major

German title: 'Mir aus den Augen'.
Text: Adam Mickiewicz.

For details of the publication of Op. 74, see **32**.

MSS. (1) Emily Elsner's album (partially destroyed): Society of Music, Warsaw.
(2) Maria Wodzińska's album: State Collection, Warsaw.
(3) Fair copy: State Collection, Warsaw (lost in 1939).

49

NOCTURNE in C sharp minor (*Lento con gran espressione*). Spring 1830.

Publication:
M. Leitgeber, Poznan (M.L.18), 5 January 1875.

Republished by:
    E. Ascherberg, London (971), 1894.
This publication was edited by Natalie Janotha, after the reproduction in facsimile of MS. (3) below, in the *Echo Muzyczne*, Warsaw, 1894. The facsimile was reproduced on the cover of this edition.

Leitgeber published the Nocturne with three mazurkas (31 and 16) with a preface by M. Szulc. It was entitled: *Trzy Mazury i Adagio utwory młodosci Fryderyka Chopina* ('Three Mazurkas and Adagio. Juvenilia of Frédéric Chopin'). *Adagio* was a generic term for any slow movement: the tempo was printed *Lento con gran espressione*.

On Brahms' copy of this publication, in the possession of Antony van Hoboken, Ascona, he has crossed out this Adagio and added 'bleibt weg' ('leave out'). This is the reason for its omission from the Breitkopf & Haertel *Gesamtausgabe*. Brahms also crossed through the preface by Szulc.

At the head of Leitgeber's publication of the *Adagio* appear the words: 'Siostrze Ludwice dla wprawy, nim się zabierze do mego drugiego Koncertu' ('For my sister Louise to play, before she practises my second concerto'). Chopin sent a copy of the nocturne to his family from Vienna in 1830, written in minute writing, in one of his letters, and may have indicated there that it was for his sister. But this letter was destroyed in the events at the Zamojski Palace in 1863, and there is no means of substantiating this very dubious inscription.[1]

In Poland the work is sometimes called the 'Reminiscence' Nocturne, because of its self-quotations from the Second Concerto (in F minor) and from the song 'Życzenie' ('The Wish'). The title was first given to the facsimile reproduction of MS. (3) in the Warsaw *Echo Muzyczne* (see above).

MSS. Three of the four manuscripts of this Nocturne listed below are extant (the whereabouts of one of them is at

[1] See *Monthly Musical Record*, November–December 1956.

present unknown), but they do not agree in detail. They are given here in the probable chronological order.

(1) One leaf, both sides written on. Unpublished. This is probably the first genuinely authentic autograph of Chopin. It is remarkable in that certain passages show an extraordinary combination of 3/4 and 4/4 tempi, very unusual for its day. A facsimile reproduction is given in *Chopin in der Heimat*, Cracow, 1955. Museo de Chopin, La Cartuja, Valldemosa.

(2) Written in a letter of 1830 from Vienna and recorded in Louise's list. Destroyed in 1863, but previously copied by the family. This copy was used as the basis for Leitgeber's publication.

(3) One leaf, one side written on. A facsimile reproduction was given in the *Echo Muzyczne*; this is a copy in an unknown hand. Public Music Library, Leningrad.

(4) Two leaves, four sides written on. This is found in Maria Wodzińska's album, a copy made by Louise in 1836. The album was reproduced in facsimile by Breitkopf & Haertel, 1910 (see **51**). The first page was again reproduced by this firm in their *Das Musikbuch*, 1913, p. 66. The introductory bar of this version is as follows:

The whole of MS. (4) was again reproduced by Binental in his *Documents and Souvenirs of Chopin*, Warsaw, 1930: Chopin Institute, Warsaw.

50

TWO SONGS for voice and PF., Op. 74: nos. 4 and 7. 1830.
    No. 4. 'Hulamka' ('Szynkareczko').
           'Merrymaking' ('Serving maid, take care').
           (G Major)
    No. 7. 'Poseł' ('Błysło ranne ziółko')
           'The Envoy' ('The early herb broke forth').
           (D major)
German titles: 'Bacchanale' and 'Der Bote'.
Text of both songs: Stefan Witwicki.

For details of publication of Op. 74, see **32**.

    Liszt transcribed no. 4, 'Hulamka', for PF. Solo. 'Poseł' is mentioned by Witwicki in his letter to Chopin of 6 July 1831.

MSS. (1) No. 7, 'Poseł': State Collection, Warsaw.
      (2) Both songs: Emily Elsner's album, State Collection, Warsaw.
      (3) Both songs: Maria Wodzińska's album, State Collection, Warsaw.

51

SONG for voice and PF. 1830.
'Czary' ('To są czary, pewno czary')
'Charms' ('This is witchcraft, surely witchcraft').
(D minor)
German title: 'Liebeszauber'.
Text: Stefan Witwicki.

Publication:

Breitkopf & Haertel, Leipzig, 1910.

The publication was a facsimile reproduction of the album which Chopin had sent to Maria Wodzińska in 1836. For many years this album was accepted by scholars as in Chopin's hand, but recent investigation has shown, almost conclusively, that it is in fact in the hand of Louise, his sister. It was entitled:

Maria. Ein Liebesidyll in Tönen.
Chopin an Maria Wodzińska.

The edition contained a preface and an appendix by Kornelia Parnas, who had received the album from a niece of Maria Wodzińska's.

Costallat, Paris, 1911.

This was a similar facsimile reproduction, with French translations of the songs by Gaston Knosp. It was entitled:

Maria. Une idylle d'amour en musique.
Chopin à Maria Wodzińska.

The first true publication was in vol. XVII of the Polish 'Complete Works' of Chopin, Warsaw, 1954.

The last stanza in Chopin's autograph (MS. (3), below) is not found in Witwicki's collected poems (*Biblical Poems, Pastoral Songs, and Sundry Verses*, Paris, 1836), indicating that the composer knew the poems in a manuscript version which differed from the final text.

'Czary' was rejected from Op. 74 by Fontana as being, in his opinion, unworthy of Chopin.

MSS. (1) Fair copy: State Collection, Warsaw.
   (2) Emily Elsner's album (partially destroyed): State Collection, Warsaw.
   (3) Maria Wodzińska's album: State Collection, Warsaw.

52

INTRODUCTION in C major to the Polonaise for PF. and cello, Op. 3. April 1830.

Publication: see **41**.

Chopin wrote to Woyciechowski on 10 April 1830: 'My Polonaise with the cello, to which I added an *Adagio* Introduction specially for Kaczyński. . . .' The whole work was performed by the composer with Kaczyński at a soirée in Lewicki's house in Warsaw in April 1830.

The MS. was deposited with Mechetti in July 1831 by Chopin himself, before he left Vienna for Paris. For the Polonaise, see 41.

MS. Lost.

53

CONCERTO in E minor, for PF. and Orchestra, Op. 11. April–August 1830.

Publication:

Kistner, Leipzig (1020–2), September 1833.
M. Schlesinger, Paris (1343), June 1833.
Wessel, London (1086), May 1834.

Dedicated to Friedrich Kalkbrenner (1788–1849), German composer, pianist and teacher, resident in Paris.

The first two movements were finished by April 1830,

the whole work by 21 August 1830. Delay in copying the orchestral parts of the Concerto in F minor led to this concerto, the second in order of composition, being published first.

The Concerto was performed by the composer privately on 22 September 1830, and publicly in the Town Hall, Warsaw, on 11 October 1830. The first performance is sometimes erroneously stated to have taken place at the house of Augustus Klengel in Dresden on 23 September 1830.

Kistner's three editions are (*a*) the original form: on the title page we read 'Exécuté par l'Autor dans ses Concerts à Paris'; (*b*) the orchestral part arranged for a second piano; (*c*) the whole work arranged for PF. Solo. The main edition has the words: '. . . avec accompagnement d'orchestre ou de Quintour *ad lib*', and from correspondence between the publisher and Aristide Farrenc, Paris, it is clear that Chopin himself arranged the quintet score. (See *Fontes Artis Musicae*, 1960–2, article by Zofia Lissa.)

Wessel published the Concerto as book XXIV of his series 'Album des Pianistes de Première Force' (see **22**). He claimed that it was 'edited and fingered' by Chopin's pupil I. [*sic*] Fontana. The same claim was made for the Studies, Op. 10. There is, actually, a possibility that Chopin did authorise Fontana in the matter.

Karl Taussig's arrangement was published by Ries & Erler, Berlin, in 1866, under the title: *Grosses Konzert in e-moll*, *Op. 11*, Bearbeitet von Karl Taussig (2047).

MS. Lost.

54

THREE NOCTURNES, Op. 9. Spring 1830–1.

No. 1 in B flat minor.
No. 2 in E flat major.
No. 3 in B major.

Publication:

    Kistner, Leipzig (995), December 1832.

    M. Schlesinger, Paris (1287), Early 1833.

    Wessel, London (nos. 1 and 2: 916; no. 3: 917). June 1833.

    Dedicated to Marie Pleyel (1811–75), wife of Camille Pleyel.

    The first few bars of no. 2, in E flat major, were written on a card to Maria Wodzińska by Chopin, dated 22 September 1835. On the other side of the card he has written: 'Soyez heureuse'. In this short extract the composer has barred the music as if it were in 6/8! (State Collection, Warsaw).

    Op. 9 was published in France before Opp. 6 and 7. Schlesinger published these nocturnes in the *Album des Pianistes: 6e année*, early in 1833. The collection was called 'morceaux inédits' and among the pieces was Field's 11th Nocturne.

    The English edition, entitled *Murmures de la Seine*, was also published before Opp. 6 and 7 and carried no opus number. Wessel later reissued the work as no. 66 (1 & 2) and no. 67 (3) of his series 'L'Amateur Pianiste'.

MS. No. 2, in E flat major: State Collection, Warsaw.

55

TWO NOCTURNES from Op. 15. Spring 1830–1.[1]

No. 1 in F major.
No. 2 in F sharp major.

Publication of Op. 15:[2]

Breitkopf & Haertel, Leipzig (5502), December 1833.
M. Schlesinger, Paris (1529), January 1834.
Wessel, London (1093), May 1834.

Dedicated to Ferdinand Hiller (1811–85), German composer and pianist, resident in Paris from 1828 to 1835. A copy of the Paris edition, in the possession of Antony van Hoboken, Ascona, is inscribed by Chopin: 'A son ami, Ferdinand, Fevrier 1834'.

Breitkopf & Haertel sent copies of their publication to Chopin in December 1833.

Schlesinger's publication is in the *Album des Pianistes*: 7e *année*, January 1834. It contains a portrait of Chopin by Pierre Roche Vigneron.

---

[1] In the opinion of Arthur Hedley, the three nocturnes of Op. 15 were composed later than this – in fact, after Chopin's arrival in Paris.
[2] The original Op. 15 was undoubtedly the 'Grand Duo' on themes from *Robert le Diable*. It was actually published thus in Germany (see **70**).

The English edition was entitled *Les Zéphirs*. Wessel later reissued the work as no. 68 of his series 'L'Amateur Pianiste'.

For Op. 15 : no. 3, the Nocturne in G minor, see **79**.

MS. Lost.

56

WALTZ in E minor. (? May) 1830.

Publication:

    J. Kauffmann, Warsaw (. . .), 1868.
    B. Schott's Sons, Mainz (19,551), 1868.

Schott's Sons issued an arrangement for PF. Duet shortly after the publication of the Waltz.

Chaberski, Cracow, published the E minor Waltz in 1871, soon after his publication of the E major Waltz (**44**).

This may be the waltz referred to by Chopin in his letter of 15 May 1830 to Woyciechowski: 'I meant to send you a new waltz to amuse you, but you shall have it next week' (but see **44**).

MS. Lost. Occasional fingering in the first edition suggests that Kauffmann used Chopin's autograph.

57

TWO STUDIES from Op. 10. (? summer) 1830.

> No. 5 in G flat major.
> No. 6 in E flat minor.

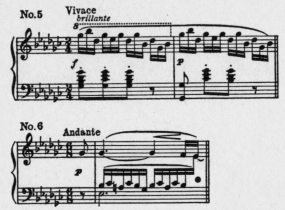

Publication:

> For details, see **42**.

No. 5, in G flat minor, is the 'Black Key' Study; the name is partly authorised by Chopin himself; see his letter to Julian Fontana of 25 April 1839.

MSS. Both Studies: State Collection, Warsaw (formerly in the Deutsche Staatsbibliothek, Berlin).

Lost work of 1830:

> WALTZ in A flat major (? December).

The Waltz may be the one referred to by Chopin in his letter of 21 December 1830 from Vienna to his family: 'I wanted to send you a waltz I have composed, but it is late now; you shall have it afterwards.' It is given in Louise's list, with the date, and so was evidently a possession of the Chopin family *c.* 1854.

58

GRAND POLONAISE in E flat major, for PF. and Orchestra, Op. 22. September 1830 to July 1831.

Publication:

> Breitkopf & Haertel, Leipzig (5709), August 1836.
> M. Schlesinger, Paris (1926), August 1836.
> Wessel, London (1643), Ent. Sta. H. 30 May 1836.

Dedicated to Mme la Baronne d'Est, sister of Pauline de Noailles, pupil of Chopin's.

In a letter of 18 September 1830 to Woyciechowski, Chopin wrote: 'I have begun a Polonaise with the orchestra.' The work was first performed in Paris on 26 April 1835 at the 'Société des Concerts du Conservatoire', in François Habeneck's 'Benefit Concert' (Habeneck was the founder of the concerts).

The Introduction – *Andante spianato* – was composed later, but published at the same time as the Polonaise (see 88).

On the French edition, Mori & Lavenu are given as the English publishers; this is an error, and probably represents an unsuccessful bid for the publication of the work. Wessel published the work as book XXXIV of the 'Album des Pianistes de Première Force' (see 22). His arrangement for PF. Solo appeared in July 1838.

MS. State Collection, Warsaw.

59

TWO STUDIES from Op. 10. Late autumn 1830.
  No. 1 in C major.
  No. 2 in A minor.

For details of the publication of Op. 10, see **42**.

MSS. (1) First writing down of no. 2, in A minor, signed
        by the composer and called 'Étude': Rudolf
        Nydahl (Stiftelsen Musikkulturens Främjande),
        Stockholm.
     (2) Fair copy of both studies, entitled 'Exercice 1 and
        2', the second one dated 'November 2, 1830'; a
        copy in the hand of Louise Chopin: State
        Collection, Warsaw (formerly with the Deutsche
        Staatsbibliothek, Berlin).

60

FOUR MAZURKAS, Op. 6. Vienna, late 1830.
  No. 1 in F sharp minor.
  No. 2 in C sharp minor.
  No. 3 in E major.
  No. 4 in E flat minor.

Publication:

Kistner, Leipzig (996), December 1832.

M. Schlesinger, Paris (1341), August 1833.

Wessel, London (958), August 1833.

Dedicated to Mlle la Comtesse Pauline Plater. The Plater family were exiled compatriots and close friends of the composer's.

These are possibly the mazurkas referred to by Chopin in a letter of 21 December 1830 to his parents: 'I don't send the mazurkas because they are not copied yet; they are not for dancing.'

Breitkopf & Haertel, in their 'Thematic Catalogue' of the works of Chopin (Leipzig, *c.* 1856, a later, revised edition of the 1852 issue), include under 'Doubtful Compositions' an arrangement of no. 1, in F sharp minor, with an Introduction in A major, dedicated to Dr H. Mumm. This mazurka was published by Kistner *c.* 1853.

The English edition of Op. 6 and those of Opp. 7, 17, 24 and 30 were all entitled *Souvenirs de la Pologne.* Wessel reissued Op. 6 later as no. 8 in his series 'L'Amateur Pianiste' (*c.* 1846).

The French edition of these mazurkas included, as a fifth mazurka, Op. 7: no. 5, in C major. For this edition, see also **25**.

MSS. (1) No. 2, in C sharp minor, first sketch (about 36 bars): Musée Adam Mickiewicz, Bibliothèque Polonaise, Paris. It was given to the poet's son, Ladislas, by Fontana, who has added the date of Chopin's death.

    (2) Fair copy of No. 2: Rudolf Nydahl (Stiftelsen Musikkulturens Främjande), Stockholm.

    (3) No. 3, in E major, in an autograph album: Rudolf Kallir and Walter Benjamin, U.S.A.

    (4) No. 4, in E flat minor, together with a first sketch of the Mazurka on the reverse side: Manuscript Department of the Public State Library, Leningrad.

61

FIVE MAZURKAS, Op. 7. Vienna, 1830–1.

    No. 1 in B flat major.

    No. 2 in A minor (2nd Version).

    No. 3 in F minor.

    No. 4 in A flat major (comp. 1824).

    No. 5 in C major.

Publication:

Kistner, Leipzig (997). December 1832.

M. Schlesinger, Paris. August 1833.

Wessel, London (959). August 1833.

Dedicated to M. Johns of New Orleans. Paul Emile Johns, an Austrian, migrated to New Orleans in 1822. He died in Paris 10 August 1860. He was commended by Chopin to Hiller as 'a distinguished amateur of New Orleans'.

For the first version of no. 2, in A minor, see **45**. For particulars of no. 4, in A flat major, see **7**.

In Schlesinger's first edition, no. 5, in C major, was omitted. See **60**.

Wessel reissued Op. 7 as no. 9 in his series 'L'Amateur Pianiste'.

Op. 7: no. 1 was published in Warsaw in 1834 as 'Ulubiony Mazur' ('Favourite Mazurka'). Friedrich Kalkbrenner's 'Variations brillantes pour le PF. sur une Mazurka de Chopin' is based on Op. 7: no. 1.

MSS. (1) No. 1, in B flat major: Rudolf Floersheim (Louis Koch Collection), Muzzano-Lugano. A facsimile of this MS. is given in Adolf Weissmann's *Chopin*, Berlin, 1912; it was reproduced, as were all of Weissmann's facsimile reproductions, from a bookseller's catalogue, in this case from the catalogue of C. G. Boerner, Leipzig, May 1908. It is an earlier version than the published one and contains minor variants.

(2) No. 3, in F minor: (*a*) a copy signed 'Vienna, F. F. Chopin, 20.6.1831'. Rudolf Floersheim (Louis Koch Collection), Muzzano-Lugano. (*b*) a copy dated 'Vienna. 20.7.1831'. Presented by its owner Louis Koch to the Russian cellist 'J. Pl.' (?). (*c*) a copy undated: Rudolf Nydahl (Stiftelsen Musikkulturens Främjande), Stockholm. It was formerly in the Kistner archives, Leipzig. There is a

facsimile reproduction in the German edition of Niecks's biography, *Chopin als Mensch und Musiker*, Leipzig, 1889.

(3) No. 4, in A flat major: see 7.

62

WALTZ in E flat major, Op. 18. Vienna, 1831.

Publication:

> Breitkopf & Haertel, Leipzig (5545), July 1834.
> M. Schlesinger, Paris (1599), June 1834.
> Wessel, London (1157), Ent. Sta. H. 30 August 1834.

Dedicated to Mlle Laura Horsford. Her name appears on early editions (not Wessel's), up to *c.* 1855, as 'Harsford'. It was corrected from her sister's name. She was the daughter of General George Horsford (see **80**) and later became Mrs Laura Lowther.

The composer sent a copy of this publication to Maria Wodzińska (see **95**). In his letter of 18 July 1834 to her brother Feliks, Chopin wrote: 'I take the liberty of sending to my estimable colleague, Mlle Maria, a little waltz which I have just published.' He inscribed the printed copy with the words: 'To Mlle Maria with respects from her former teacher' ('Hommage à Mlle M. W. de la part de son ancien professeur! F. F. Chopin. 18 jui. 1834'). The month, which could be 'juin' or juillet', has been wrongly interpreted as June. That it is, in fact, July, is clear from the beginning of the letter above (and see **86**). The inscribed copy is in the State Collection, Warsaw. Maria had sent Chopin a set of variations composed by herself.

The manuscript of this work was originally bought by Pleyel (see Niecks, 1, p. 273), who may actually have engraved the music before selling his stocks to Schlesinger (see 76). The copyright of the work was sold by Schlesinger to Henri Lemoine, Paris, at the end of 1844.

The English edition was entitled *Invitation pour la Danse* and the waltz became widely known in England as 'L'Invitation'. Wessel later reissued the waltz as no. 28 in his series 'L'Amateur Pianiste', and again in a *Collection of German Waltzes*.

MSS. (1) State Collection, Warsaw.

     (2) Mariemont Museum, Belgium.

     (3) Archives of Count Paul de la Panouse, Yvelines: see 92.

63

THREE SONGS for voice and PF., Op. 74: nos. 3, 15 and 16. Vienna, 1831.

No. 3 'Smutna Rzeka' ('Rzeko z cudzoziemców strony')
      'The sad stream' ('A stream flowing from foreign
      parts')
               (F sharp minor)

German title: 'Trübe Wellen'.

Text: Stefan Witwicki.

MS. Lost.

No. 15 'Narzeczony' ('Wiatr zaszumiał . . .')
      'The Bridegroom' ('The wind rose . . .')

German title: 'Die Heimkehr'.
Text: Stefan Witwicki.

MS. State Collection, Warsaw.

No. 16 'Piosnka litewska' ('Bardzo raniuchno')
'Lithuanian Song' ('Very early in the morning').
(F major)

German title: 'Lithuanisches Lied'.
Text: Ludwik Osiński.

MSS. (1) Musée Adam Mickiewicz, Bibliothèque Polonaise, Paris (first sketch).
(2) Memorial Library of Music, Stanford University, California (see **12**). Copy in another hand.
(3) Maria Wodzińska's album: State Collection, Warsaw.

For details of the publication of Op. 74, see **32**.

64

WALTZ in A minor, Op. 34: no. 2. Vienna, 1831.

Publication:

> Breitkopf & Haertel, Leipzig (6033), December 1838.
> M. Schlesinger, Paris (2716), December 1838.
> Wessel, London (2281), Ent. Sta. H. 1 December 1838.

Dedicated to Mme la Baronne C. d'Ivri.

The opus was published as *Trois Valses Brillantes*, Op. 34. (For the other two waltzes of Op. 34: no. 1, in A flat major, see **94**; no. 3, in F major, see **118**.)

Schlesinger published the waltzes in the *Album des Pianistes*, announced on 15 November 1838.

Wessel's edition was published in the series 'Le Pianiste Moderne', no. 96.

MSS. (1) Dated 'Vienna, 1831': whereabouts unknown.
(2) Fragment (title page): Society of Music, Warsaw.

65

SCHERZO no. 1, in B minor, Op. 20. Vienna, May–June 1831; revised Paris, 1832.

Publication:

Breitkopf & Haertel, Leipzig (5599), March 1835.

M. Schlesinger, Paris (1832), February (–April) 1835.

Wessel, London (1492), August 1835.

Dedicated to M. Thomas Albrecht, wine merchant, attaché to the Saxon Legation in Paris, and one of the composer's warmest friends.

The Trio (not so called by Chopin) in B major is based on the Polish Christmas folk-tune 'Lulajże Jezuniu' ('Lullaby, little Jesus').

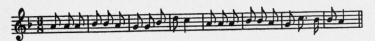

The English edition is entitled *Le Banquet Infernal*. Wessel reissued the work later as no. 56 in his series 'L'Amateur Pianiste'.

The French edition was presented first as an exclusive supplement for subscribers to Schlesinger's journal *Gazette Musicale*. It was on sale normally two months later.

MS. Lost.

66

BALLADE no. 1, in G minor, Op. 23. Vienna, sketched May–June 1831; completed Paris, 1835.

Publication:

Breitkopf & Haertel, Leipzig (5706), June 1836.

M. Schlesinger, Paris (1928), July 1836.

Wessel, London (1644), Ent. Sta. H. 30 May 1836.

Dedicated to M. le Baron de Stockhausen, Hanoverian Ambassador to France (father of Elisabet Herzogenberg, the friend of Brahms).

The disputed E flat in the tenor part of bar 7 is unmistakable in MS. (1) below, reproduced in the *Revue Musicale*, December 1931.

Breitkopf & Haertel published the Ballade separately, but also, at the same time, included it in an *Album Musical*, containing a miscellany of songs and PF. pieces by Loewe, Liszt, Spohr, Mendelssohn, etc. In the *Album* Chopin's work was entitled 'Ballade ohne Worte'.

The work is sometimes called the 'Polish' Ballade. The English edition was entitled *Ballade ohne Worte*, or *La Favorite Ballade*. Wessel reissued the work as no. 69 in his series 'L'Amateur Pianiste'.

Schumann's remark, '... sein genialischtes (nicht genialstes) Werk', was written of this Ballade.

MSS. (1) Gregor Piatigorsky, U.S.A. (incomplete).

(2) Last two staves in an album: Marc Loliée, Paris (*c.* 1953).

67

STUDY in C minor, Op. 10: no. 12. (? September) 1831.

For details of the publication of Op. 10, see 42.

The work is the so-called 'Revolutionary' Study and is supposed to have been inspired by the downfall of Warsaw in September 1831, the news of which reached the composer at Stuttgart. There is no particle of evidence for this most firmly entrenched legend in the Chopin literature, and as with other nicknamed works of the composer its attributed date is therefore not to be relied on.

MSS. (1) Rudolf Nydahl (Stiftelsen Musikkulturens Främ-jande), Stockholm.

(2) Nine bars (nos. 9–17), written in the album of George Sand, and with the indication *appassionato*: Nicolas Rauch, Geneva, November 1957.

68

STUDY in C major, Op. 10: no. 7. Spring 1832.

For details of the publication of Op. 10, see 42.

The piece was placed eleventh in the original ordering.

MS. Pierpont Morgan Library, New York (formerly in the Ernest Schelling Collection) (two pages).

69

CONTRABASS PART to a three-part canon in B minor by Mendelssohn, 16 April 1832

Mendelssohn called his Canon 'à 3', but his bass part is in strict canon with the three upper parts. Chopin's addition is not to be taken seriously: a free, florid parody written in the empty bars of Mendelssohn's bass stave.

The MS. contains this remark by Mendelssohn: 'Contra basso libro composti di Sciopino [i.e. Chopin]. La basso est à vous. Felix Mendelssohn-Bartholdy. Paris 16.4.32.'

The page is reproduced in facsimile in Binental's *Documents and Souvenirs of Chopin*, Warsaw, 1930.

MS. Originally in the possession of Mme Laura Ciechowska, Warsaw, whose collection was destroyed in the Second World War.

70

GRAND DUO in E major, on themes from Meyerbeer's *Robert le Diable*, for PF. and cello. No opus number. Early 1832.

Publication:

A. M. Schlesinger, Berlin (1777) (as 'Op. 15'), July 1833.
M. Schlesinger, Paris (1376), 6 July 1833.
Wessel, London (1085), December 1833.

The work was composed in collaboration with Auguste Joseph Franchomme (see **160**). In his letter of 12 December 1831 to Woyciechowski, Chopin wrote: '... Schlesinger... has engaged me to write something on themes from *Robert le Diable*, which he has bought from Meyerbeer for 24,000 francs.'

Amongst the themes used, the chief ones are:

(*a*) the 'Romanza', Act i;

(*b*) the Chorus 'Non v'è pietà', Act i;

(*c*) the Terzetto 'Le mie cure, ancor dal cielo', Act v.

Robert le Diable was first performed at the Paris Opéra on 21 November 1831.

The Duo was later arranged by Chopin and Franchomme as a PF. Duet and this was published by A. M. Schlesinger (2238) in 1838; it was given the opus number '15'.

Wessel called this Duo, on publication, 'Op. 12', substituting it for the real Op. 12 – the variations on a theme from Hérold (see **80**).

A PF. Duet arrangement was also published by Schlesinger in Paris in February 1839 (2799) and called 'Op. 15'.

MS. Conservatoire, Paris.

71

MAZURKA in D major. 1832.

Allegro ma non troppo

Publication:

Breitkopf & Haertel, Leipzig (*Gesamtausgabe*, vol. XIII, no. 7), January 1880.

This is a considerably revised version of the Mazurka in D major, of 1829 (**31**).

MS. Lost.

72

Allegro de Concert in A major, Op. 46. Sketched in 1832, revised and completed in May 1841.

Publication:

    Breitkopf & Haertel, Leipzig (6651), December 1841.
    M. Schlesinger, Paris (3481), November 1841.
    Wessel, London (5298), Ent. Sta. H. 20 January 1842.

Dedicated to Friederike Müller, a favourite pupil of Chopin's, who became an eminent Austrian pianist. She married Johann Baptiste Streicher, the Viennese pianoforte manufacturer. Her letter of thanks to the composer, sent from Vienna, is dated 21 December 1841.

It seems fairly clear that the work was originally conceived as a PF. Concerto, the material possibly dating from as early as 1830 when Chopin, in Vienna, had discussed the composition of a concerto for two pianofortes to be played by himself and a friend (and schoolfellow) Thomas Nidecki. Either this, or fresh material, was worked on in 1832 for the first movement of a PF. Concerto. His father mentioned this projected work in a letter of 1834, and wrote again on 11 April 1835: 'You don't mention whether you have finished your third concerto' – words which probably refer to this proposed work. The music was taken up again in the spring of 1841 after a promise to Friederike Müller to compose a concert piece for her. The 'Allegro de Concert' is thus a pastiche of early work in which the original *soli* and *tutti* passages are still distinguishable. That the composer always thought of it as a concerto is clear from his letter to

Fontana of 16 October 1841, in which he wrote of it by that name (see **142**).

An arrangement of the piece for PF. and Orchestra, by Jean Louis Nicode (1835–1919), a pupil of Kullak, and like the composer himself a Pole of French extraction, was published by Breitkopf & Haertel in 1880. He added 79 spurious bars.

MSS. (1) Biblioteka Narodowa (National Library), Warsaw (originally in the possession of Breitkopf & Haertel).

    (2) Heinemann Foundation, New York. This is a fair copy made by Fontana; it contains the dedication 'à Mlle F. Müller (de Vienna)'.

73

MAZURKA in B flat major. 24 June 1832.

Publication:

    Lamus (a periodical), no. 2, Lwow, 1909.

The work, twenty-two bars long, was composed for Mme Alexandra Wołowska, wife of 'Wołowski, the deputy', as he is called by Chopin's friends. It was written in her album, which was discovered in the posthumous papers of the Kátýl family, Polish refugees living in Paris, by Dr Stanisław Lam.

    There is a facsimile reproduction of the *Lamus* publication in Maria Mirska's book *Szlakiem Chopina*, Warsaw, 1935.

MS. Jasieński Museum, Lwow.

74

STUDY in E major, Op. 10: no. 3. 25 August 1832.

For details of the publication of Op. 10, see **42**.

The study was originally marked *vivace* and there was no later direction *poco più animato*. The tempo was subsequently changed to *Lento ma non troppo*.

MSS. (1) First version with several important variants, dated 'Paris, 25 August 1832': Robert Owen Lehman Foundation, Washington.

(2) Fair copy: State Collection, Warsaw (formerly with the Deutsche Staatsbibliothek, Berlin). This MS. is marked *vivace ma non troppo*.

MS. 1 was presented, together with the manuscript of **75**, to Friederike Müller by the composer.

75

STUDY in C sharp minor, Op. 10: no. 4. August 1832.

For details of the publication of Op. 10, see **42**.

MS. Dated 'Paris, August 1832': Rudolf Floersheim, Muzzano-Lugano, Switzerland (Louis Koch Collection). This MS., together with that of Op. 10: no 3, was presented by the composer to Friederike Müller in April 1841 (see 74 and 72).

76

INTRODUCTION AND RONDO in E flat major, Op. 16. 1832.

Publication:

> Breitkopf & Haertel, Leipzig (5525), March 1834.
> Ignace Pleyel, Paris (16), December 1833.
> Wessel, London (1143), Ent. Sta. H. 30 August 1834.

Dedicated 'à son élève, Mlle Caroline Hartmann.' Caroline Hartmann (1808–34), daughter of a cotton manufacturer of Münster, and admired as a child prodigy by Spohr, was a pupil of Chopin and Liszt. She afterwards became a well-known pianist and composer.

The *andante* Introduction is in C minor.

The French edition was advertised by Pleyel, together with Op. 17, in the *Gazette Musicale*, 23 March 1834. Soon afterwards Pleyel's stocks were bought by Schlesinger and others. Schlesinger's edition of Op. 16 appeared in June 1834 (1703).

Wessel's edition appeared under the title: 'Rondoletto sur le Cavatina de *L'Italiana in Algeri*' – a claim without foundation. His PF. Duet arrangement, published in October 1837, was called *Rondo Elégante*. He reissued the work later as no. 24 of his series 'L'Amateur Pianiste'.

Breitkopf & Haertel's edition gives Pleyel, Paris, as the publisher of the French edition.

MS. Lost.

77

Four Mazurkas, Op. 17. 1832–3.
No. 1 in B flat major.
No. 2 in E minor.
No. 3 in A flat major.
No. 4 in A minor.

Publication:

Breitkopf & Haertel, Leipzig (5527), March 1834.
Ignace Pleyel, Paris (2912), December 1833.
Wessel, London (1144), Ent. Sta. H. 30 August 1834.

Dedicated to Mme Lina Freppa, a teacher of singing. She was born in Naples of French extraction, separated from her husband and living in Paris. She was a friend of Chopin and Bellini, and a favourite with both composers.

Mazurka no. 4, in A minor, may have been first sketched in 1824 (see **8**).

Schlesinger's edition of Op. 17 (1704) appeared in June 1834 (see note to previous item).

Wessel's edition of Op. 17 is dedicated to Mme Lina

Treppa (*sic*). He reissued the work as no. 27 in his series 'L'Amateur Pianiste'. On the English edition, Schlesinger is given as the Paris publisher, but the German edition gives Pleyel. Both the Pleyel editions of Opp. 16 and 17 are in the possession of Alan Tyson, London.

MS. (inscribed 'F. Chopina – T. Kwiatkowsky') Jagiellonian Library, Cracow.

78

Six Studies from Op. 25. 1832–4.

    No. 4 in A minor.
    No. 5 in E minor.
    No. 6 in G sharp minor.
    No. 8 in D flat major.
    No. 9 in G flat major.
    No. 10 in B minor.

Publication of Op. 25:

> Breitkopf & Haertel, Leipzig (two parts: 5832-3),
> October 1837.
>
> M. Schlesinger, Paris (2427), October 1837.
>
> Wessel, London (two parts: book I, 1832; book II,
> 1833), October 1837.

Dedicated to Marie, Comtesse d'Agoult (1805-76),
French authoress ('Daniel Stern'), mother, by Liszt, of
Cosima, Wagner's second wife.

No. 6, in G sharp minor, is the 'Thirds' Study; no. 8, in
D flat major, is the 'Sixths' Study; no. 9, in G flat major, is
the 'Butterfly-wings' Study; no. 10, in B minor, is the
'Octaves' Study.

Schlesinger's copyright was sold to Henri Lemoine, Paris, in early 1842 (Lemoine's PN is 2776).

Wessel's edition numbers the studies of Op. 25 as if they continued the series in Op. 10, i.e. book 1 contains nos. 13–18 and book 11 nos. 19–24.

MSS. (1) Complete manuscript of Op. 25 (originally with Breitkopf & Haertel): Chopin Institute, Warsaw. Nos. 1 and 8 only are in Chopin's hand; but the whole MS. was revised by him.

    (2) Nos. 4, 9 and 10: Lost (formerly with Édouard Frank).

    (3) No. 4, in A minor: Bibliothèque de l'Opéra, Paris.

79

NOCTURNE in G minor, Op. 15 : no. 3. 1833.

For details of the publication of Op. 15, see **55**.

The album supplement to Schlesinger's *Gazette Musicale*, entitled *Album des Pianistes: annee 7e*, containing the three nocturnes of Op. 15, and with a portrait of Chopin by Vigneron as a frontispiece, was sent by Chopin to his sister Louise early in 1834, that is, soon after its publication. The album also contains treatments by various composers contemporary with Chopin of the 'Ronde' theme from Hérold's *Ludovic* on which he himself had written variations (see next). Louise's copy, beautifully bound, was formerly with the late Arthur Hedley.

The story that Chopin wrote on the MS. of this G minor Nocturne 'After a performance of *Hamlet*' is almost certainly an invention.

MS. Lost.

80

INTRODUCTION AND VARIATIONS in B flat major, in the 'Ronde' theme from Hérold's *Ludovic*, Op. 12. Summer 1833.

Publication:

> Breitkopf & Haertel, Leipzig (5495), November 1833.
> M. Schlesinger, Paris (1499), January 1834.
> Cramer, Addison & Beale, London (?),[1] 1834.

Dedicated to Mlle Emma Horsford, a pupil of Chopin, and the daughter of General George Horsford, sometime Lieutenant-Governor of the Bermudas. She later became Mrs Emma Appleyard. (See **62**.)

Hérold died while working on *Ludovic* and the opera was completed by Fromental Halévy. The first performance of

---

[1] No copy seen by the author.

Ludovic took place in Paris on 16 May 1833. The theme is from Act 1, no. 2, the 'Ronde favori':

> Je vends des scapulaires,
> Et de pieux rosaires . . .

for soprano solo and chorus. The key of the piece is also B flat major. Chopin's introduction is followed by four variations.

The theme was also made the basis of variations by Pixis, Hünten and Herz, and their work was published in the album supplement containing Chopin's Op. 15 (see previous item).

The *Ludovic* variations were not included in Wessel's English edition; instead the 'Grand Duo Concertante' for PF. and cello (**70**), which has no opus number, was substituted, and called 'Op. 12'.

The German edition was the first publication by Breitkopf & Haertel of a work by Chopin.

The French edition was announced as early as July 1833.

MS. Lost.

81

INTRODUCTION AND BOLERO in A minor and major, Op. 19. 1833.

Publication:
>   C. F. Peters, Leipzig (2505), October 1834.
>   Prillip, Paris (237: see note below), early 1835.
>   Wessel, London (1491), Ent. Sta. H. 21 April 1835.

Dedicated to Mlle la Comtesse Émilie de Flahault.

The Introduction is in C major.

The English edition was entitled *Souvenir d'Andalousie*. It was issued as no. 54 of the series 'L'Amateur Pianiste'. The Paris publisher is given by Wessel as Phillip, but the variants in the spelling of this name, even in Paris itself, are very numerous.

Prillip's first edition has no publisher's number; it was added to later editions. Pleyel intended to publish the Bolero. His publication is announced in the archives of the Paris 'Depôt Légal' under 1 November 1834. Prillip was a successor to Pleyel, acquiring part of his stocks in 1834. The French edition, together with Op. 20, was reviewed in the *Gazette Musicale*, 22 March 1835.

MS. Sketch (incomplete) for the first version: Conservatoire, Paris. This sketch was published in the *Journal de Musique*, Paris, no. 8, 22 July 1876, under the fictitious title: 'Chanson de Zingara: Souvenir du voyage en Espagne' (see 33).

82

MAZURKA in C major. 1833.

Publication:

    J. Kauffmann, Warsaw (171), 1870.

    B. Schott's Sons, Mainz (20,030), 1870.

This Mazurka may have been intended for the publisher Schuberth, Hamburg, who, in September 1833, advertised an *Original-Bibliothek für PF.*, to contain pieces by modern composers. Among the names is Chopin's.

MS. Lost.

83

STUDY in A minor, Op. 25 : no. 11. 1834.

For details of the publication of Op. 25, see **78**.

This is the 'Winter Wind' Study. The four opening bars were added after the study was composed, on the suggestion of Charles A. Hoffmann.

MS. See **78**.

84

'CANTABILE' in B flat major. 1834.

Publication:

Muzyka, nos. 4–6, Warsaw (edited by Ludwik Bronarski), 1931.

The piece, fourteen bars long, was reproduced in facsimile in the *Album von Handschriften berühmter Persönlichkeiten von Mittelalter bis zur Neuzeit*. This volume, published by Rudolf Geering, Basel, in 1925, was a collection of autograph facsimiles, in the possession of the late Karl Geigy-Hagenbach (now of his heirs) in Basel.

MS. Signed 'F. F. Chopin, Paris, 1834': unknown.

85

MAZURKA in A flat major. July 1834.

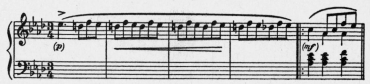

Publication:

> Gebethner & Wolff, Warsaw (edited by Maria Mirska) (6905), 1930. The edition gives a facsimile of the manuscript.

The manuscript carries the heading 'Paris 1834'. It was inserted in an album which had belonged to Maria Szymanowska, the celebrated Polish pianist, pupil of John Field and beloved by Goethe; she died in 1831 at St Petersburg. The Mazurka was probably placed in her album by her daughter, Celina, who came to Paris in July 1834 to marry Adam Mickiewicz, the poet and a friend of Chopin's. There seems little doubt that the Mazurka was written for Celina Szymanowska, although there is no dedication to her on the manuscript.

The next facsimile reproduction was in *Die Musik*, Berlin, vol. XXIII, no. 6, March 1931. There was also a reproduction of the first page in the catalogue of the 'Frédéric Chopin Exposition' arranged by the Bibliothèque

Polonaise, Paris, in 1932. The whole Mazurka, forty-two bars long, was again reproduced in facsimile in *Szlakiem Chopina*, by Maria Mirska, Warsaw, 1935.

MSS. (1) Musée Adam Mickiewicz, Bibliothèque Polonaise, Paris.

     (2) Album leaf, the edges highly decorated, an exact copy in Chopin's hand: Museo de Chopin, La Cartuja, Valldemosa.

86

PRELUDE in A flat major. 18 July 1834.

Publication:

    Pages d'Art (a periodical), Geneva, August 1918.

Republished by:

    (*a*) Henn, Geneva (244), 1919.

(?) { (*b*) Rossignol, Paris.
      (*c*) London & Continental Music Publishing Co., London.

The inscription on the autograph is to Pierre Wolff, and the date is 18 July 1834. Wolff (1810–82) was a teacher of the pianoforte in the Geneva Conservatoire and a friend of Liszt. Liszt dedicated his 'Grande Valse di bravura' (composed in 1865) to him. Chopin became acquainted with Wolff through their mutual friendship with Anton Wodziński, since the Wodziński family was, at that time, living in Geneva. Chopin, in his letter of 18 July 1834 to Anton's brother, Feliks, wrote: 'So I had to wait [i.e. before answering Feliks's letter] till after the good Wolff had gone.'

The Prelude was first performed in public by E. R. Blanchet on 9 April 1919; the republication above followed this performance.

The French and English editions, though projected, were, as far as is known, never published.

The manuscript of the Prelude passed from Wolff to his pupil Aline Forget. It was found in the family papers by Pierre Forget and from him passed to the present owners.

MS. (not entitled 'Prelude'): Spokane University, Spokane, Washington, U.S.A.

87

FANTASIE-IMPROMPTU in C sharp minor, Op. 66 (Posth.) 1835.

Publication:

    A. M. Schlesinger, Berlin (4392), May 1855.

    J. Meissonnier Fils, Paris (3523), July 1855.

    Ewer & Co., London (no PN), (?).

Meissonnier's editions of the posthumous works were published without opus numbers.

Dedicated to Mme d'Esté.

The reason why Chopin withheld this piece from publication is not known. Arthur Hedley (*Chopin*, London, 1947) suggests that the theme bore too close a resemblance to Moscheles' 'Impromptu in E flat', Op. 89. This Impromptu was included in the album containing Chopin's Op. 15 (see **55**). Another explanation was put forward by Ernst Oster, 1947, according to whom Chopin felt that his theme bore too close a resemblance to the finale of Beethoven's Op. 27: no. 2, the 'Moonlight' Sonata, and therefore would not publish it.

Before the discovery of the original manuscript the attributed date was 1834 – given by Fontana. It has been suggested that he added the prefix 'Fantasie' to Chopin's original title of 'Impromptu'. The work was first played by Marcellina Czartoryska in Paris, March 1855.

MS. Album belonging to Mme d'Este. The piece is headed 'Composé pour Mme la Baronne d'Este par F. F. Chopin. Paris, Vendredi, 1835': Artur Rubinstein (sold in Paris 10 June 1960). A copy by Marcellina Czartoryska, entitled 'Impromptu inédit par Frédéric Chopin'; Unknown.

88

ANDANTE SPIANATO in G major, for PF. Solo, Op. 22. 1834.

For details of the publication of Op. 22, see **58**.

This work, although for PF. Solo, was composed as an

introduction for the Polonaise in E flat major when this was published as Op. 22. The whole work appeared as *Grande Polonaise Brillante précédée d'un Andante Spianato.*

Wessel published the work as book XXXIV of the 'Album des Pianistes de Première Force'. The French edition gives the English publishers, erroneously, as Mori & Lavenu (see **58**).

MS. State Collection, Warsaw. It is inscribed to Maria Wodzińska with whom, in the autumn of 1835, Chopin had become reacquainted.

89

FOUR MAZURKAS, Op. 24. 1834-5.
    No. 1 in G minor.
    No. 2 in C major.
    No. 3 in A flat major.
    No. 4 in B flat minor.

Publication:
    Breitkopf & Haertel, Leipzig (5647), January 1836.
    M. Schlesinger, Paris (1870), January 1836 (see note).
    Wessel, London (1645), Ent. Sta. H. 20 April 1836.

Dedicated to M. le Comte de Perthuis, an aide-de-camp of Louis Philippe, *officier d'ordonnance.*

No. 3, in A flat, may possibly have been sketched in Warsaw before 1831 (see MS. (2), below).

Wessel reissued the work as no. 80 in his series 'L'Amateur Pianiste'.

The French edition was announced in November 1835 and published in the supplement *Album des Pianistes: annee 8e* on 25 December 1835.

MSS. (1) The whole opus: National Library (Biblioteka Narodowa), Warsaw.

(2) No. 3, in A flat, inscribed by Chopin 'à Mme Linde', but dated '22 September 1835' (see **10**): Society of Music, Warsaw.

90

TWO POLONAISES, Op. 26. 1834–5.
No. 1 in C sharp minor.
No. 2 in E flat minor.

Publication:

Breitkopf & Haertel, Leipzig (5707), July 1836.
M. Schlesinger, Paris (1929), July 1836.
Wessel, London (1647), Ent. Sta. H. 30 May 1836.

Dedicated to Josef Dessauer (1798–1876), born in Prague, and an ardent, not untalented, composer. He lived in Paris from 1833 to 1834, and again from 1840 to 1842. Dessauer was a friend of George Sand, who portrayed him in her play *Maître Favilla*.

Schlesinger's edition was published as a supplement for subscribers to his journal *Gazette Musicale*, 31 July 1836.

The English edition was entitled *Les Favorites*. Wessel reissued the work as no. 83 in his series 'L'Amateur Pianiste'.

Some editions, e.g. Jurgenson's, edited by Karl Klindworth, and Wessel's, omit the vital *da capo* from the end of the first polonaise, in C sharp minor.

MS. Pierpont Morgan Library, New York.

91

NOCTURNE in C sharp minor, Op. 27: no. 1. 1835.

Publication:

Breitkopf & Haertel, Leipzig (5666), May 1836.
M. Schlesinger, Paris (1935), July 1836.
Wessel, London (1648), Ent. Sta. H. 30 May 1836.

Op. 27 was dedicated to Mme la Comtesse d'Apponyi, wife of the Austrian Ambassador to France. Comtesse d'Apponyi, née Therese Nogarola – the 'divine Therese' – was frequently hostess to Chopin.

For Op. 27: no. 2, see **96**.

Schlesinger's edition had been advertised the previous December.

The English edition of the opus was entitled *Les Plaintives*. Wessel reissued it later as no. 84 in his series 'L'Amateur Pianiste'.

MS. Together with Op. 27: no. 2, Schott's Sons, Mainz.

92

WALTZ in G flat major, Op. 70 (Posth.): no. 1. 1833.

For details of the publication of Op. 70, see **40**.

The date 1835 had been given by Fontana. There were sketches for the Waltz, almost indecipherable, among the papers of the Chopin family, *c.* 1855, and these must date from before 1831.

MSS. (1) Sketches originally with the Chopin family: unknown.

    (2) Conservatoire, Paris (together with **35**).

    (3) Marked *leggieramente*, and differing from (2): Archives of Comte de la Panouse, Yvelines (discovered in 1967). The MS. was donated to the family by Chopin in 1833.

93

TWO MAZURKAS, Op. 67 (Posth.). 1835.
    No. 1 in G major.
    No. 3 in C major.

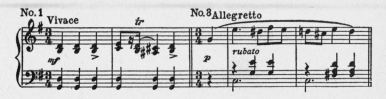

Publication of Op. 67:

    A. M. Schlesinger, Berlin (4393), May 1855.

    J. Meissonnier Fils, Paris (3524), July 1855.

Meissonnier's editions of the posthumous works were published without opus numbers.

No. 1, in G major, was written for Mlle Młokosiewicz; see Chopin's letter to Fontana of 7 October 1841.

No. 3, in C major, was written for Mme Hoffman. Mme Klementyna Hoffmann, nee Tańska, an authoress, was the wife of the French author Charles A. Hoffmann.

For Op. 67: no. 2, see **167**; for Op. 67: no. 4, see **163**.

MS. Lost.

94

Waltz in A flat major, Op. 34: no. 1. Tetschen, 15 September 1835.

Publication:

    Breitkopf & Haertel, Leipzig (6032), December 1838.

    M. Schlesinger, Paris (2715), December 1838.

    Wessel, London (2280), Ent. Sta. H. 1 December 1838.

Dedicated to Mlle de Thun-Hohenstein, daughter of a wealthy and cultured family at Tetschen (Czech: Děčín), friends of the composer. Tetschen is a town on the way from Prague to Dresden, in Bohemia, where Chopin stayed with the Thun-Hohenstein family during September 1835. For Op. 34: no. 2 and Op. 34: no. 3, see **64** and **118**.

MSS. (1) Inscribed 'à Mlle J. de Thun': in an album belonging to the family and dated 15 September 1835. This version agrees closely with the published one.

(2) A fair copy, originally with Breitkopf & Haertel: Society of Music, Warsaw. This contains only bars 1 to 80, but it has Chopin's dedication written on it – 'à Mlle J. de Thun-Hohenstein'.

95

WALTZ in A flat major, Op. 69 (Posth.): no. 1 ('L'Adieu' Waltz). Dresden, 24 September 1835.

* This note is dotted in M S (1)
** d♭ in M S (1)
† c in M S (1)

Publication:

A. M. Schlesinger, Berlin (4395), May 1855.
J. Meissonnier Fils, Paris (3526), July 1855.
See also note to the dedication below and also note to MS. (3).

Meissonnier's editions of the posthumous works were published without opus numbers.

Dedicated to Maria Wodzińska (1819–96), who was a sister of boyhood friends of the composer (Anton, Casimir and Feliks). She and the composer became reacquainted in September 1835 and he fell in love with her. A member of her family, Count Wodziński, wrote the biographical novel *Trois Romans de Frédéric Chopin*, Paris, 1886, in which the waltz is, for the first time, reproduced in facsimile. The composer has written on the autograph 'pour Mlle Marie' and added the date and place. Maria entitled her copy 'L'Adieu'.

A copy in the Chopin family papers appears in Louise's list, dated by her '1836'.

The Waltz is often wrongly designated in catalogues and concert programmes as being in F minor.

For Op. 69: no. 2, the Waltz in B minor, see **35**.

MSS. (1) Maria's copy: State Collection, Warsaw.

(2) Copy inscribed by the composer 'à Mme Peruzzi: hommage de F. F. Chopin, 1838': Harvard University, Dumbarton Oaks, U.S.A. Mme Peruzzi was the wife of the Ambassador of the Duke of Tuscany to the French Court.

(3) Copy inscribed by the composer 'à Mlle Charlotte de Rothschild: hommage de F. F. Chopin, Paris, 1841': Conservatoire, Paris. There are variants in this copy. It was reproduced in facsimile in the periodical *Peuple Amis*, Paris, 1949, p. 55, and was first published in the *Oxford Edition of Chopin's Works*, London, 1932, vol. 1.

(4) Copy made by Auguste Franchomme for Jane Stirling, on 22 May 1850: Jagiellonian Library, Cracow University. There are further variants in this copy.

96

NOCTURNE in D flat major, Op. 27: no. 2. Autumn 1835.

For details of the publication of Op. 27, see **91**.

Mendelssohn wrote to his family from Leipzig on 6 October 1835: 'He [Chopin] has such a pretty new nocturne.'

MSS. (1) Biblioteka Narodowa (National Library), War-saw. (This manuscript, originally with Breitkopf & Haertel, carries an indication '8e Nocturne' crossed through by Chopin. It was, in fact, the eighth nocturne to be published.)

(2) Both nocturnes: Schott's Sons, Mainz.

97

STUDY in F minor, Op. 25: no. 2. January 1836.

For details of the publication of Op. 27, see **78**.

MSS. (1) First sketch, dated '27 January 1836'; the tempo marking is *Presto agitato*: Museo de Chopin, La Cartuja, Valldemosa.

(2) Fair copy, written at Dresden and dated '1836',

with the marking *agitato*: State Collection, Warsaw (together with Op. 25 : no. 1).

(3) Fair copy, together with Op. 25 : no. 1 : Chopin Institute, Warsaw. This manuscript, originally with Breitkopf & Haertel, has 'pour être publié 15 Octobre' on the title-page.

98

STUDY in C sharp minor, Op. 25 : no. 7. Early 1836.

For details of the publication of Op. 25, see **78**.

MSS. (1) Unknown, formerly with Édouard Frank.
　　　(2) Whole MS., see **78**.

99

TWO STUDIES, from Op. 25. 1836
　　　No. 3 in F major.
　　　No. 12 in C minor.

For details of the publication of Op. 25, see **78**.

Schumann refers to no. 12, in C minor, as 'a late one'.

MSS. (1) No. 3, in F major: unknown, formerly with Édouard Frank.

(2) Whole MS., see **78**.

(3) No. 12 in C minor. Written in an album of musical autographs belonging to the Cheremetieff family and dated 'Paris, 20 May 1845': Manuscript Department of the Lenin State Library, Moscow.

100

TWO PRELUDES, from Op. 28. 1836.

No. 7 in A major.

No. 17 in A flat major.

For details of the publication of Op. 28, see **107**.

The date of the A major Prelude is known from the fact that Chopin wrote it in Delphine Potocka's album in 1836.

The A flat Prelude is also of this period. In his note of 1837 to Fontana, Chopin wrote: '. . . copy out the A flat Prelude for me; I want to give it to Perthuis' (see **89**).

MSS. (1) No. 7, in A major: Delphine Potocka's album (see **35**).

(2) The same: Chopin Institute, Warsaw, in a manuscript volume containing all the Preludes.

(3) No. 17, in A flat major: Gesellschaft der Musikfreunde, Vienna. This belonged to Clara Schumann. She bequeathed it to Brahms, from whom it passed to its present owners. It is a doubtful autograph, and may be the copy made by Fontana (above).

(4) The same: Chopin Institute, Warsaw, in a manuscript volume containing all the Preludes.

(5) The same: eight bars, inscribed 'Paris, 9 November 1839 de la part de l'ami F. F. Chopin', written in the album of Ignaz Moscheles: Sotheby, London, 8 December 1959.

101

SONG for voice and PF., Op. 74: no. 17. 1836.

'Śpiew grobowy' ('Leci liście drzewa')

'Hymn from the Tomb' ('The leaves drift from the tree').

(E flat minor)

German title: 'Polens Grabgesang'. English title: 'Poland's Dirge'.

Text: Wincenty Pol.

For details of the publication of Op. 74, see **32**.

The 'Hymn from the Tomb' was published later than the rest of Op. 74, *c.* 1872, by Schlesinger of Berlin. (1872: incorporated with the other sixteen songs of Op. 74; 1873: as a separate song.) Fontana's intention was to include only sixteen songs in Op. 74, since, as he recalled in his letter of 1835 to Chopin's sister Louise, the composer had had a superstitious dread of the number 7.

An arrangement of the song for PF. Solo, called 'Chant de Tombeau', made by Rudolf Hasolf, appeared from Schlesinger in 1861 (PN 5139) and was called 'Op. 75'. At the same time a PF. Duet version (PN 5140) was also published. These PF. arrangements preceded the publication of the song itself. The English edition of Stanley Lucas & Weber (1874) gives this 'Hymn from the Tomb', but in Peters' edition (1887) it is omitted.

It has been stated, but without any documentary evidence, that the song was composed by Chopin actually on 3 May 1836 – the 'Third of May' which commemorates the founding of Poland's constitution.

MS. Lost.

> A copy used by Schlesinger is in the possession of Antony van Hoboken, Ascona; it is not in Fontana's hand. He had no copy, in fact, in 1855 during his preparations for Op. 74.[1]

102

BALLADE no. 2, in F major, Op. 38, First version: 1836; final version: Majorca, January 1839.

[1] See the *Musical Quarterly*, New York, January 1956.

Publication:

Breitkopf & Haertel, Leipzig (6330), October 1840.
Troupenas, Paris (925), September 1840.
Wessel, London (3555), Ent. Sta. H. 1 October 1840.
Dedicated to Schumann.

The work is said to be based on ideas from the poem 'Świteź' by Adam Mickiewicz.[1]

The composer rarely played the whole Ballade; this may account for Schumann's remarks that when he heard Chopin play it at Leipzig in 1836 the middle section (*presto con fuoco*) and the coda (*agitato*) were missing and therefore composed later.

The English edition is entitled: *La Gracieuse*.

Chopin wrote to Fontana in April 1840: 'Troupenas has bought my seven compositions and will do business with Wessel direct.' This Ballade is the earliest of the seven works to which the composer refers; the others are:

(*a*) SONATA in B flat minor, Op. 35;
(*b*) IMPROMPTU in F sharp minor, Op. 36;
(*c*) TWO NOCTURNES, G minor and G major, Op. 37;
(*d*) SCHERZO in C sharp minor, Op. 39;
(*e*) TWO POLONAISES, A major and C minor, Op. 40;
(*f*) FOUR MAZURKAS, E minor, C sharp minor, B major and A flat major, Op. 41.

MSS. (1) Rudolf Nydahl (Stiftelsen Musikkulturens Främjande), Stockholm (formerly with Ernst Rudorff and Peters' Musikbibliothek, Leipzig).

(2) Conservatoire, Paris. At the end of this manuscript, p. 9, in another hand, are the words: 'A mon cher Ch. Ritter, P. Seligmann bien heureux de lui offrir ce MS. de F. Chopin.'

---

[1] See *Chopin's Musical Style*, Gerald Abraham, London, 1960 ed., p. 57 n.

103

SONG for voice and PF., Op. 74: no. 14. Dresden, 8 September 1836.

'Pierścień' ('Smutno niańki ci śpiewały')
'The Ring' ('Thy nurses sing sadly for thee').

German title: 'Das Ringlein'.
Text: Stefan Witwicki.

For details of the publication of Op. 74, see **32**.

The four-bar prelude given in some editions is not authentic. Liszt transcribed the song for PF. Solo, published by Schlesinger, 1860 (see **32**).

MSS. (1) State Collection, Warsaw. It is inscribed 'Drezno, 8 7bre 1836'.
(2) Another copy, previously owned by Fontana: on sale in Paris, November 1959.

104

STUDY in A flat major, Op. 25: no. 1. Dresden, early September 1836.

For details of the publication of Op. 25, see **78**.

This is the 'Shepherd-boy' Study.

An autograph copy of the study was sent to Clara Schumann (née Wieck) accompanied by a note from the composer: 'à Mlle Clara Wieck par con admirateur. Leipzig, 12 September 1836.' This note was kept by a later owner together with a MS. of the Polonaise in A flat, Op. 53 **(147)**. This fortuitous association led to the supposition that Chopin was offering the Polonaise to Clara Schumann and the erroneous conclusion then drawn that the Polonaise had been written, or at least sketched, as early as 1836.

MSS. (1) Fair copy, together with Op. 25: no. 2, in F minor: State Collection, Warsaw. This copy is headed 'Dresden, 1836'.

(2) Fair copy, together with the F minor Study: Chopin Institute, Warsaw (see **97**).

(3) Complete MS. of the studies: see **78**.

105

FOUR MAZURKAS, Op. 30. 1836–7.

No. 1 in C minor.
No. 2 in B minor.
No. 3 in D flat major.
No. 4 in C sharp minor.

Publication:

Breitkopf & Haertel, Leipzig (5851), January 1838.

M. Schlesinger, Paris (2489), January 1838.

Wessel, London (2170), Ent. Sta. H. 21 November 1837.

Dedicated to Mme la Princesse de Württemberg (*née* Czartoryska).

No. 4 in C sharp minor, was sketched earlier than 1836.

The opus was presented to readers of the Paris *Gazette Musicale* as a supplement on 25 March 1838.

MS. (Copy in another hand): Biblioteka Narodowa (National Library), Warsaw.

106

TWO NOCTURNES, Op. 32. 1836–7.

No. 1 in B major.

No. 2 in A flat major.

Publication:

A. M. Schlesinger, Berlin (2180), December 1837.

M. Schlesinger, Paris (2500), December 1837.

Wessel, London (2169), Ent. Sta. H. 21 November 1837.

Dedicated to Mme la Baronne de Billing, *née* Camille de Courbonne, a pupil of Chopin's and on intimate terms with him, enough to call him, in a letter, a 'charmant sylphe'.

A. M. Schlesinger included the second Nocturne in an *Album des Pianistes*, no. 2. This was a collection 'inédites, modernes et brillantes', published in late 1837, although dated 1838.

The English edition was entitled *Il lamento e la consolazione*.

MS. Lost.

107

SEVENTEEN PRELUDES, from Op. 28. 1836 to November 1839.

No. 3 in G major.   No. 15 in D flat major.
No. 5 in D major.   No. 16 in B flat minor.
No. 6 in B minor.   No. 18 in F minor.
No. 8 in F sharp minor.   No. 19 in E flat major.
No. 9 in E major.   No. 20 in C minor.
No. 11 in B major.   No. 22 in G minor.
No. 12 in G sharp minor.   No. 23 in F major.
No. 13 in F sharp minor.   No. 24 in D minor.
No. 14 in E flat minor.

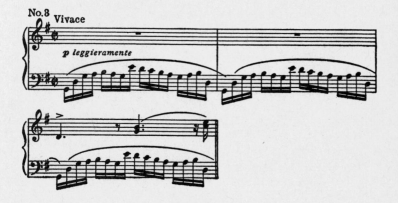

Publication:

Breitkopf & Haertel, Leipzig (6088: cahiers I and II), September 1839

Adolphe Catelin, Paris (560), June 1839.

Wessel, London (book I: 3098; book II: 3099), Ent. Sta. H. 30 August 1839.

The French and English editions were dedicated to Camille Pleyel (1788–1855), pianist, composer, publisher and PF. manufacturer.

The German edition was dedicated to Joseph Christoph Kessler (1800–72), Bohemian pianist and composer, an acquaintance of Count Potocki. Kessler's twenty-four Preludes, Op. 31, had been dedicated to Chopin. This German edition gives 'Paris, chez Pleyel et Cie' for the French publishers.

The French edition, published in two parts, carried no opus number; this is because Chopin, in a letter to his publisher, written from Marseilles in March 1839, was unable to recall it. The absence of an opus number on the Preludes persisted in France for long after Chopin's death (till *c.* 1860). Schlesinger's successor in the business, Brandus, purchased the copyright of the Preludes from Catelin, *c.* 1844.

The English edition likewise carried no opus number and was also published in two parts, Wessel entitling them the 5th and 6th books of *Studies*. He announced the publication of them in October 1839. Later, apparently, '28' was added to the blank opus number, but on book II only.

The reservation of the number '28' for these Preludes on publication (by June 1839 the composer's opus numbers had reached 34) suggests that the idea of publishing a collection of preludes had been in Chopin's mind from the time that Op. 27 had been published, at the end of 1835, and that in all probability the composition of some of them had been begun by then.

(*a*) No. 8, in F sharp minor, was believed by Liszt to be the Prelude inspired by the rainstorm at Valldemosa (see (*d*) below).

(*b*) No. 9, in E major, was transcribed by Liszt for Organ Solo and published by Schuberth, Leipzig, in Gottschalg's *Repertorium für Orgel*, no. 8, *c*. 1864.

(*c*) No. 14, in E flat minor, carries in most editions the direction *Allegro*. Édouard Ganche, in his *Oxford Edition* of the composer's works (London, 1932), states that in Jane Stirling's copy of the Prelude (the French edition) Chopin himself emended the word to *Largo*.

(*d*) No. 15, in D flat major, is the 'Raindrop' Prelude. Both it and no. 6, in B minor, have been claimed as the music which George Sand mentioned in her description of the rainstorm at Valldemosa.[1]

(*e*) No. 20, in C minor: the disputed note in the last chord of bar 3, given in most editions as E natural, is stated by Ganche (loc. cit.) to be E flat, since Chopin had pencilled in a flat before the printed E in Jane Stirling's copy.

See also **100, 123, 124**. For the Prelude in A flat, see **86**; for the Prelude in C sharp minor, Op. 45, see **141**.

[1] See *Musical Times*, London, August 1957.

MSS. The complete set of Preludes: Biblioteka Narodowa
(National Library), Warsaw. The manuscript, Chopin's
fair copy made from existing sketches and fair copies,
shows many alterations. These may be due to last-
minute revisions or to mistakes in copying afterwards
corrected. It bears the dedication, in Chopin's hand,
to J. C. Kessler, but the manuscript went to Catelin,
Paris, and not to Breitkopf & Haertel. The German
publishers received Fontana's copy of the Preludes.
This copy by Fontana, frequently mistaken for an
autograph of Chopin's, is in private possession.

108

NOCTURNE in C minor. 1837.

Publication:

Towarzysto Wydawnicze Muzyki Polskiej ('Society for the
Publication of Polish Music'), no. 83, Warsaw, Spring
1838. Edited by Ludwik Bronarski, together with the
Largo in E flat major (**109**).

Attention was first drawn to this unpublished work, and
to the *Largo* in E flat, by an article in the *Polski Rocznik
Muzykologiczny* ('Polish Musicological Annual'), Warsaw,
1937.

The piece, forty-five bars long, may be a rejected item
from Op. 32. It was later republished by Alfred Cortot
in 'L'Edition de travail des *Œuvres Posthumes* de Chopin'.

MSS. (1) Sketch of the opening bars, differing from the final version, and

(2) Final version, fair copy:

Both MSS. in the Conservatoire, Paris.

109

LARGO in E flat major. (?) 1837.

Publication:

> *Towarzysto Wydawnicze Muzyki Polskiej*, no. 83, Warsaw, Spring 1838 (see previous item).

The manuscript of the work, sixteen bars long, is simply dated '6 July' and the year of composition is unknown. If its association in the Paris Conservatoire Library with the previous item gives any grounds for believing that it is of the same period, then the work may be a rejected Prelude. Its style faintly resembles that of the prelude in the same key, Op. 28: no. 20.

MS. Conservatoire, Paris.

110

IMPROMPTU no. 1, in A-flat major, Op. 29. 1837.

Publication:

Breitkopf & Haertel, Leipzig (5850), January 1838.

M. Schlesinger, Paris (2467), October 1837.

Wessel, London (2166), Ent. Sta. H. 14 October 1837.

Dedicated to Mlle la Comtesse de Lobau.

The English edition was called 'Op. 28' for many years. It was advertised, as on sale, in the *Musical World*, 20 October 1837.

Schlesinger's edition was published as a supplement for subscribers to his journal *Gazette Musicale*, 29 October 1837.

MS. State Collection, Warsaw (formerly with the Deutsche Staatsbibliothek, Berlin).

111

SCHERZO no. 2, in B flat minor, Op. 31, 1837.

Publication:

Breitkopf & Haertel, Leipzig (5852), February 1838.

M. Schlesinger, Paris (2494), December 1837.

Wessel, London (2168), Ent. Sta. H. 21 November 1837

Dedicated to Mlle la Comtesse Adèle de Fürstenstein.

Wessel entitled his edition *Le Méditation*.

MSS. (1) Chopin Institute (a copy in another hand).
    (2) Conservatoire, Paris (given after Chopin's death by his sister Louise to Thomas Tellefsen).

112

SONG for voice and PF., Op. 74: no. 12. 1837.

'Moja pieszczotka' ('Moja pieszczotka, w gdy wesołej')
'My Darling' ('My darling, when you are happily singing').

(G flat major)

German title: 'Meine Freuden'.

Text: Adam Mickiewicz.

For details of the publication of Op. 74, see **32**.

Liszt transcribed this song for PF. Solo (see **32**).

MS. Sketch, in A flat major: Cracow Music Society. On the
MS. Chopin has written 'w Ges trzeba śpiewać'
('transpose into G flat'). The successive owners of the
MS. have written their names on it: T. Kwiatowski,
1872; Marcelline Czartoryska; Stanisław Tarnowski,
26 February 1885. There is a facsimile of the MS. in
Binental's *Documents and Souvenirs of Chopin*, Warsaw,
1930.

113

VARIATION no. 6, in E major (Largo) for the *Hexameron*.
1837.

Publication:

> Tobias Haslinger, Vienna (7700), 1839.
> Bernard Latte, Paris (?), 1839.
> Cramer & Co., London (406), 1839.

Dedicated to Mme la Princesse Christine de Belgiojoso.

The *Hexameron* was a collection of six variations for PF. Solo on the March in Bellini's opera *I Puritani di Scozia* contributed by Liszt, Thalberg, Pixis, Herz, Czerny and Chopin. The Introduction, bridge passages and Finale were composed by Liszt, who also arranged a shortened version for two pianofortes, published by Schuberth, Leipzig, in 1870. (The version for PF. and Orchestra is not by Liszt.) The variations were published as: '*Hexameron*, Morceau de Concert. Grandes Variations de Bravoura pour Piano sur le Marche des Puritains de Bellini.' It was composed for the Princess de Belgiojoso, who wished to raise money from its sales for impoverished Polish exiles. It was first performed in 1837 (a date wrongly given on occasion as the date for its publication).

The Vienna edition gives Mori & Lavenu as the English publishers: this is an error.

Vincenzo Bellini (1801–35): the first performance of *I Puritani* took place in the Théâtre-Italien, Paris, on 24 January 1835.

MS. Lost.

114

FUNERAL MARCH from the Sonata no. 1, in B flat minor, Op. 35. 1837.

Marche funèbre

pp pesante e sostenuto   *p*

For details of the publication of Op. 35, see **128**.

The movement was composed first, but only published with the complete sonata. Following the news of Chopin's death, Wessel of London, Troupenas of Paris and Breitkopf & Haertel of Leipzig simultaneously published the March as an independent composition on 17 November 1849.

MS. The complete Sonata: Chopin Institute, Warsaw (possibly a copy in the hand of Fontana).

115

FOUR MAZURKAS, Op. 33. 1837–8.
    No. 1 in G sharp minor.
    No. 2 in D major.
    No. 3 in C major.
    No. 4 in B minor.

Publication:

    Breitkopf & Haertel, Leipzig (5985), November 1838.
    M. Schlesinger, Paris (2714), October 1838.
    Wessel, London (2279), Ent. Sta. H. 2 November 1838.

Dedicated to Mlle la Comtesse Rosa Mostowska, daughter of the Minister of Public Information.

The original tempo on the composer's MS. of no. 1, in G sharp minor, is *Presto*. He seems, according to one or two copies in the possession of his pupils, to have changed the tempo later to *Lento*.

No. 3, in C major, is the mazurka which is supposed to have led to a quarrel between Chopin and Meyerbeer over the time-signature.

Schlesinger published these mazurkas as a supplement to his journal *Gazette Musicale*, 28 October 1838. In this supplement the C major and D major mazurkas were nos. 2 and 3 respectively.

Mazurkas nos. 1 and 2 were first published by Breitkopf & Haertel in a collection called *Album für PF. & Gesänge für 1839*. All four were then published as shown above with the PN as it had occurred in the consecutive numbering of the pieces in the *Album*.

MSS. (1) All four mazurkas, fair copy: Biblioteka Narodowa (National Library), Warsaw.
     (2) Fragments of nos. 1 and 4, with the title page:
Chopin Institute, Warsaw.

Fontana's copies of the four mazurkas were sold by Leo Liepmannssohn, Berlin, in May 1930. They are now separated and in the possession of the following:

1. There is a facsimile of the greater part of this copy in Adolf Weissmann's *Chopin*, Berlin, 1912. In this copy the key-signature has only four sharps, and it is printed thus in the German edition: unknown.

2. The greater part of this copy of no. 2 was reproduced in the 'Mazurkas' volume of the Breitkopf & Haertel edition of Chopin's works, edited by Ignaz Friedmann, 1929: Robert Owen Lehmann Foundation, Washington.

3. The copy of no. 3 (headed by Chopin 'no. 2') was discovered in 1968 and is now in the Academy of Music, Tokyo.

4. No. 4, in B minor: Library of Congress, Washington.

116

SONG for voice and PF., Op. 74: no. 2. 1838.

'Wiosna' ('Błyszczą krople rosy mruczy zdrój po błoni')
'Spring' ('The dew glistens, the stream gushes through
the fields').

(G minor)

German title: 'Frühling'.
Text: Stefan Witwicki.

For details of the publication of Op. 74, see **32**.

Liszt transcribed the song for PF. Solo (6 *Chants polonaise*,
no. 2), published by A. M. Schlesinger, Berlin, 1860. For
Chopin's own arrangement for PF. Solo, see next.

MSS. (1) City Library, Kornik (formerly with Baron L.
Kronenburg, Warsaw).

(2) The voice part, with words added, and dated
'1 September, 1848', written in the album of Miss
Fanny Erskine: Fitzwilliam Museum, Cambridge.
(Miss Erskine was a niece of Jane Stirling.)

117

ANDANTINO in G minor: an arrangement for PF. Solo of
the song 'Wiosna' ('Spring'), Op. 74: no. 2. Six manuscripts:
April 1838 to 1 September 1848.

Publication:

Schott, London (6708), July 1968.

The edition was edited by Ateş Orga, and also contained the two bourrées, **160**(B). There is a facsimile of MS. (3) in the publication.

MSS. (1) This version, the earliest, is dated April 1838: unknown.

(2) A version written on both sides of an album leaf, with mauve borders, inscribed at the end 'à Madame Kiéré, hommage respectueux de son dévoué Chopin': Sotheby, London, 17 June 1958. Mme Kiéré was a Parisian hostess and a friend of Fanny Herschel, sister of Mendelssohn.

(3) A version signed by the composer and dated 'Paris, 5 February 1846': Gesellschaft der Musik-freunde, Vienna (presented by Count Victor Wimpffen, in 1898). The title *Andantino* and ' "Wisona": Paroles de Witwicki' have been added by another hand. There is a reproduction of this MS. in *Chopin und Wien*, Franz Zagiba, Vienna, 1951.

(4) A version, dated 4 September 1847, Paris, dedicated to 'dear Teofil Kwiatowski'. It is signed by Chopin and the dedicatee. The tempo is *Lento*: Stargardt, Marburg, 19 February 1969.

(5) A version, dated 'London, 28 June 1848', written in minute writing for a miniature album belonging to Mrs S. Horsley: unknown.[1]

(6) A version dated 'Manchester, 1 September 1848': Kórnik Library.

118

WALTZ in F major, Op. 34: no. 3. 1838.

[1] For particulars of this album, see *Mendelssohn and his Friends in Kensington*, ed. Rosamund Brunel Gotch, Oxford University Press, London, 1938, p. 50 n.

Publication:

Breitkopf & Haertel, Leipzig (6034), December 1838.
M. Schlesinger, Paris (2717), December 1838.
Wessel, London (2282), December 1838.

Dedicated to Mlle A. d'Eichtal, daughter of Baron d'Eichtal, and a pupil of Chopin's. At the house of Baron d'Eichtal Charles Hallé first heard Chopin play. The composer wrote in his letter of April 1839 to Fontana: '... tell me whether you took a waltz from me to Mlle Eichtal.'

The three waltzes of Op. 34 were included by Schlesinger in an *Album des Pianistes* announced on 15 November 1838 in the *Gazette Musicale* as consisting of new and unpublished pieces (with portraits of the composers) by Thalberg, Chopin, Doehler, Liszt, Osborne and Mereaux. Amédée Mereaux's contribution was a 'Fantasia on a Mazurka by Chopin'.

Chopin was annoyed by the use of his waltzes for this *Album*: see his letter to Fontana of 28 December 1838.

This waltz in F major is the so-called 'Cat' Waltz. For Op. 34: no. 1, see **94**; for Op. 34: no. 2, see **64**.

MS. Lost.

119

NOCTURNE in G minor, Op. 37: no. 1. 1838.

Publication:

Breitkopf & Haertel, Leipzig (6334), June 1840.
Troupenas, Paris (893), June 1840.
Wessel, London (3554), Ent. Sta. H. 19 June 1840.
There is no dedication of Op. 37. For the Nocturne in G major, Op. 37: no. 2, see 127
The English edition is entitled *Les Soupirs*.

MS. Biblioteka Narodowa (National Library), Warsaw, together with 127. This manuscript, originally with Breitkopf & Haertel, is not in Chopin's hand, although possibly corrected by him.

120

POLONAISE in A major, Op. 40: no. 1. October 1838.

Publication:

Breitkopf & Haertel, Leipzig (6331), December 1840.
Troupenas, Paris (977), December 1840.
Wessel, London (3557), November 1841.

Dedicated to Julian Fontana (1810–69), a friend and fellow-pupil of Chopin's at the Warsaw Conservatoire. After 1830, he, like Chopin, settled in Paris.

He asked Chopin to alter the middle section of this Polonaise and the composer replied: 'I will alter the second half of the Polonaise for you until I die.' It had been Chopin's intention to dedicate this Polonaise to Titus Woyciechowski, and its companion, Op. 40: no. 2, to Fontana. The inscription on the autograph runs: '2 Polonaises dédiés à T. W. / son ami Julius Fontana', but on publication the 'T. W.' was omitted (MS. (2) below).

For Op. 40: no. 2, see next.

Wessel called the two Polonaises of Op. 40 *Les Favorites*, as he had Op. 26.

MSS. (1) British Museum, together with Op. 40: no. 2. These autographs were the basis of Troupenas' edition. (It was Chopin's practice, to save the bother of writing out repeats, to letter the bars alphabetically and then leave a corresponding number of blank bars, each bearing its appropriate letter. In this MS. the 15th bar of the 'Trio' section bears the letter 'p' (Chopin omitted 'j'). This was misinterpreted by Troupenas as 'piano' and reproduced in subsequent editions. This fact was first pointed out by Dr Oswald Jonas, Chicago.)

(2) (Thaddeus Jentysie): this autograph was found in his posthumous papers, its present whereabouts unknown. The first page was reproduced in facsimile in the *Echo Muzyczne*, Warsaw, October 1899, the fiftieth anniversary of Chopin's death. The whole MS. was reproduced in Binental's *Chopin: Life and Art*, Warsaw, 1937.

(3) Biblioteka Narodowa (National Library), Warsaw (together with Op. 40; no. 2) – a copy in another hand.

121

POLONAISE in C minor, Op. 40: no. 2. Sketched October 1838, finished Majorca, early 1839.

For details of the publication of Op. 40, see previous item.

The opening theme has been compared to that of Kurpiński's 'Coronation' Polonaise, set to the words 'Hail! O King!' and written for Nicolas I, 1826. Chopin's theme is claimed to be a minor-key variant:

MSS. (1) British Museum, together with Op. 40: no. 1.

     (2) Biblioteka Narodowa (National Library), Warsaw (copy in another hand).

122

MAZURKA in E minor, Op. 41: no. 2. Majorca, 28 November 1838.

Publication of Op. 41:

    Breitkopf & Haertel, Leipzig (6335), December 1840.

    Troupenas, Paris (978), December 1840.

    Wessel, London (3558), Ent. Sta. H. 9 December 1840.

For the other three mazurkas of Op. 41, see **126**.

Dedicated to Étienne (= Stefan) Witwicki.

MSS. (1) Gregor Piatigorsky, Los Angeles (former owners: Pauline Viardot-Garcia and Henry Fatio). The MS. is headed 'Palma. 28 9br'. At the foot of the first page is a sketch of the Prelude in E minor, Op. 28: no. 4. On the next page are sketches for the Prelude in A minor, Op. 28: no. 2, and for two other preludes, afterwards rejected, in B flat major and C sharp minor. (L. Bronarski, *Music Manuscripts of Chopin at Geneva*, Cracow, 1930.)

(2) Incomplete version: Conservatoire, Paris.

(3) Gesellschaft der Musikfreunde, Vienna; possibly a copy by Fontana, but signed by Chopin.

123

FOUR PRELUDES from Op. 28. Palma, Majorca, November–December, 1838.

No. 2 in A minor.
No. 4 in E minor.
No. 10 in C sharp minor.
No. 21 in B flat major.

For details of the publication of Op. 28, see **107**.

Liszt transcribed no. 4, in E minor, for organ solo.

MSS. Sketches of nos. 2 and 4, see previous item. For the inclusion of nos. 10 and 21, see also previous item. All the preludes: Biblioteka Narodowa (National Library), Warsaw.

124

PRELUDE in C major, Op. 28: no. 1 (?) Majorca, January 1839.

For details of the publication of Op. 28, see **107**.

There is a tradition that this was the last prelude to be composed.

MS. All the preludes: Biblioteka Narodowa (National Library), Warsaw.

125

SCHERZO in C sharp minor, Op. 39. Begun at Majorca, January 1839, finished mid-1839.

Publication:

Breitkopf & Haertel, Leipzig (6332), November 1840.

Troupenas, Paris (926), December 1840.

Wessel, London (3556), Ent. Sta. H. 1 October 1840.

Dedicated to Adolf Gutman (1819–82), German pianist and composer, pupil of Chopin.

The work is referred to by Chopin in his letter to Fontana of 17 March 1839 as still unfinished; it was played to Moscheles in the autumn of that year by Gutman.

MS. Chopin Institute, Warsaw. The MS., originally with Breitkopf & Haertel, is inscribed by the composer to 'Gustman'.

126

THREE MAZURKAS from Op. 41. July 1839.

For details of the publication of Op. 41, and for Mazurka no. 2, in E minor, see 122.

The order of the mazurkas in the opus is not standardised. In the thematic catalogue devised for Jane Stirling by

Chopin and Franchomme, the order is (1) E minor, (2) B minor, (3) A flat major, (4) C sharp minor; this may well be the order of composition. See Chopin's letter of August 1839 to Fontana.[1]

MS. All four mazurkas: Chopin Institute, Warsaw. This is the MS. used by Breitkopf having the mazurkas in the order (1) A flat major, (2) C sharp minor, (3) E minor, (4) B major.

127

NOCTURNE in G major, Op. 37: no. 2. July 1839.

For details of the publication of Op. 27, see 119.

MS. Biblioteka Narodowa (National Library), Warsaw, together with Op. 27: no. 1 (copy in another hand).

128

SONATA no. 1, in B flat minor, Op. 35 (first movement, Scherzo and Finale). Summer 1839.

---

[1] In this letter, the original of which was owned by Arthur Hedley, Chopin writes quite distinctly of the first Mazurka as being in C (*sic*) minor. This may, of course, be a slip of the pen.

FINALE

Publication:

>Breitkopf & Haertel, Leipzig (6329), May 1840.
>Troupenas, Paris (891), May 1840.
>Wessel, London (3549), July 1840.

There is no dedication of Op. 35.

The slow movement ('Funeral March') had been composed in 1837, see **114**.

A copy of the French edition, inscribed by Chopin to Jane Stirling, is in the Jagiellonian Library, Cracow University.

The Sonata was edited by Brahms for the Leipzig *Gesamtausgabe* (vol. VIII, 1878).

MS. Chopin Institute, Warsaw. This manuscript, originally with Breitkopf & Haertel, is a copy in another hand.

129

IMPROMPTU no. 2, in F sharp major, Op. 36. Early autumn 1839.

Publication:

>Breitkopf & Haertel, Leipzig (6333), May 1840.
>Troupenas, Paris (892), May 1840.
>Wessel, London (3550), July 1840.

There is no dedication of Op. 36.

Wessel was prevented by Chopin himself from entitling this work 'Agréments au Salon'.

MSS. (1) Fragmentary sketches: Czartoryski Museum, Cracow. These sketches are bound in with Chopin's manuscript of the 'Krakowiak' Rondo, Op. 14 (see 29).

     (2) Fragment (two pages): Chopin Institute (1960), Warsaw.

129(B)

CANON at the octave in F minor. (?) 1839.

Unpublished

The manuscript, a rough draft, consists of nineteen or so bars with many erasures and corrections.

MS. Nicolas Rauch, Geneva, November 1957.

130

TROIS NOUVELLES ÉTUDES. Late autumn 1839.
No. 1 in F minor.
No. 2 in A flat major.
No. 3 in D flat major.

Publication:

A. M. Schlesinger, Berlin (2207:2423), August–September 1840.

M. Schlesinger, Paris (2345), 15 November 1840.

Chappell, London (6084), January 1841.

The three studies were composed at the request of Ignaz Moscheles. They were published in the *Méthode des Méthodes de Moscheles et Fétis.* This was an elaborate Pianoforte 'Tutor' in three parts: the first part contained a system of elementary instruction, the second part 'Progressive Exercises', the third part a series of mostly new studies called 'Études de Perfectionnement', in which these three of Chopin's studies were included.

In Germany the work was called *Pianoforte-Schule aller Pianoforte-Schulen* and in England *Complete System of Instruction for the Pianoforte.* Part III of the English edition includes the Chopin studies as nos. 3, 4 and 5. A later English edition was published by Jullien & Co, London, with an introduction by G. A. MacFarren.

Other contributors to the 'Études de Perfectionnement' were Mendelssohn ('Étude in F minor') and Liszt ('Morceau de Salon').

The first part of the *Méthode* was published in France and Germany in 1837, which accounts for Maurice Schlesinger's publisher's number and for the earlier one of A. M. Schlesinger's German edition; the introduction to the whole work, by Fétis, is dated in the French and English editions '1 November 1840'. Chopin's three studies were issued as a separate publication in Paris and Berlin in September 1841.

A later edition of the *Méthode*, published by Brandus (M. Schlesinger's successor in the business), contains variants in all three studies which derive from Chopin himself.

Facsimile of no. 1, in F minor, with a preface by Arthur Hedley: London 1940.

MSS. (1) No. 1, in F minor, 10 bars, dated '16 January 1841', copied by Chopin into the album of the sculptor Jean-Pierre Dantan (1800–69): Bibliothèque Nationale, Paris.

(2) No. 1, in F minor, the first 23 bars, signed by the composer and dated 8 December 1841: an album once belonging to Jenny Vény and containing autographs of Liszt, Moscheles, Berlioz, etc.: Houghton Library, Harvard University, Cambridge, Mass.

(3) All three studies (Museo de Chopin, La Cartuja, Valldemosa).

131

WALTZ in A flat major, Op. 42. Spring 1840.

Publication:
> Breitkopf & Haertel, Leipzig (6419), July 1840.
> Pacini, Paris (3708), 30 June 1840.
> Wessel, London (3559), July 1840.

There is no dedication of Op. 42.

In his letter of 18 June 1840 to Breitkopf, Chopin wrote: 'As Signor Pacini is publishing a waltz of mine in the *Cent-et-un* on the 30th inst., I think it best to send you a proof.'

Cent-et-un was one of Pacini's several 'Albums', that is, serial publications issued approximately twice a month. Each issue contained a collection of works by different composers of the day. *Cent-et-un* consisted of PF. works only; it was announced in February 1838 and was to consist of twenty-five books, each to contain ten or fifteen pages. Presumably it was to end after the publication of 101 compositions, but the project was never adhered to.

Pacini wrote to Chopin on 22 April 1840 postponing the publication of this waltz, because the next number of *Cent-et-un*, he wrote, would contain works only by Cherubini and Niedermeyer. On 20 June 1840 he wrote asking Chopin for the corrected proofs, one of which, evidently, the composer had sent to Breitkopf & Haertel. The Waltz, entitled 'Grande Valse Nouvelle', Op. 42, appeared as 'no. 68 des *Cent-et-un*', pp. 408–15.

Pacini's business was purchased by Louël, Paris, *c.* 1850, and from Louël it passed finally to Simon Richault, Paris, in 1866. All Pacini's successors published the waltz with their own imprints.

Wessel entitled the waltz the 'Cent-et-un Waltz'! This incomprehensible title was later dropped.

The prompt publication of Op. 42 (Op. 41, for instance, composed a year earlier, did not appear until six months after Op. 42) may be due to the different publisher but is more probably an indication of the popularity of Chopin's waltzes.

MS. Lost.

132

SONG for voice and PF. March 1840.
   'Dumka' ('Mgła mi do oczu zawiewa z łona')
   'Reverie' ('Mist before my eyes').
                     (A minor)
Text: Bohdan Zaleski, from the poem 'Nie ma czego trzeba'.
See **156**.

Publication:

   The periodical *Słow Polskie*, Lwow, 22 October 1910,
   in an issue devoted to the centenary of Chopin's birth-
   year, edited by Stanisław Lam.

Lam discovered the song, which is eight bars long, in 2/4
time, in an album belonging to Stefan Witwicki. His
printed publication was reproduced in facsimile by Maria
Mirska in her book *Szlakiem Chopina*, Warsaw, 1935, p. 152.

MS. Lost.

133

WALTZ ('SOSTENUTO') in E flat major. 20 July 1840.

Publication:

Francis Day & Hunter, London (23,100), May 1955 (edited by Maurice J. E. Brown).

The piece, in the nature of a waltz but not so entitled, is 48 bars long and was probably written for Émile Gaillard (see **140**). It was given to its present owners by Joseph Gaillard in 1938.

MS. Conservatoire, Paris. It is signed by the composer and dated 'Paris, 20 July 1840'. 1840 is the one year in a decade when Chopin was not at Nohant, the home of George Sand, during the summer months.

134

MAZURKA in A minor (*Notre Temps*). Summer 1840.

Publication:

This mazurka was first published in 'Six Morceaux de Salon' (no. 1) by the Bureau de la *France Musicale* on 4 July 1841. Chopin's mazurka and four other pieces from this collection were then published by Schott's Sons, Mainz, in an album entitled 'Notre Temps' (6493/no. 2), in February 1842.

Republished by:

(*a*) Troupenas, Paris (978), as 'Mazurka élégante', January 1845.

(*b*) Wessel, London (6313), January 1846.

'Notre Temps' was the general title of twelve pieces composed by Czerny, Chopin, Kalliwoda, Rosenhain, Thalberg,

Kalkbrenner, Mendelssohn, Bertini, Wolff, Kontski, Osborne and Herz. Mendelssohn's contribution was the 'Prelude and Fugue in E minor'. 'Notre Temps' was on sale through agents in Leipzig (Breitkopf) and Vienna (H. F. Müller).

The French republication was advertised in the journal *La France Musicale*, 5 January 1845, as on sale at the 'Bureau Central de Musique'. Troupenas's business was bought about 1850 by Brandus.

Wessel, without authorisation, entitled his edition *The Cracow Mazurka* and he gave it the opus number '59: *bis*'.

MS. Lost.

135

POLONAISE in F sharp minor, Op. 44. Late 1840 to August 1841.

Publication:

> Pietro Mechetti, Vienna (3577), November 1841.
> M. Schlesinger, Paris (3477), November 1841.
> Wessel, London (5226, *sic*, see below). Ent. Sta. H. 20 January 1842.

Dedicated to Mme la Princesse de Beauvau (*née* Komar), a sister of Delphine Potocka (see Chopin's letter to his parents, 21 November 1830).

In his letter to Fontana of 25 August 1841, Chopin wrote: '... a new kind of Polonaise, but it is more a fantasia.' These words refer to this piece, since two days previously he had written to Mechetti, offering a 'Fantasia en forme de Polonaise' for 25 *louis d'or*.

Wessel's publisher's number is an error for '5296'.

MS. Lost.

136

BALLADE no. 3, in A flat major, Op. 47. Sketched 1840, finished summer 1841.

Publication:

> Breitkopf & Haertel, Leipzig (6652), January 1842: advertised in December 1841.
> M. Schlesinger, Paris (3486), November 1841.
> Wessel, London (5299), Ent. Sta. H. 20 January 1842.

Dedicated to Mlle Pauline de Noailles, a favourite pupil of Chopin's.

MSS. (1) Chopin Institute, Warsaw, destroyed in Second World War.

(2) Formerly with Jan Ostrowski: unknown.

137

FANTASIA in F minor, Op. 49. Sketched early in 1841, finished October 1841.

Publication:

Breitkopf & Haertel, Leipzig (6654), January 1842.
M. Schlesinger, Paris (3489), November 1841.
Wessel, London (5301, *sic*, see below), Ent. Sta. H. 20 January 1842.

Dedicated to Mme la Princesse Catherine de Souzzo, a pupil of Chopin's. The composer wrote to his family on 20 July 1845 of her mother, Princess Obreskowa: 'I have had many proofs of her kind-heartedness, and am very fond of her. She is devoted to music.' The name 'Sonzzo' in the dedication of the German edition is an error.

For his letter to Breitkopf & Haertel of 4 May 1841 mentioning this work and the 'Allegro de Concert', Op. 46, see **142**.

Wessel's publisher's number is an error for 5302; 5301 is the Nocturnes, Op. 48: no. 2 (**142**).

MS. Biblioteka Narodowa (National Library), Warsaw.

138

WALTZ in F minor, Op. 70: no. 2 (Posth.). June 1841.

For details of the publication of Op. 70, see **40**.

The Waltz may have been written earlier than 1841: in the list devised by Chopin's sister Louise, it is dated '1840–41'. It was evidently a composition kept by Chopin for private gifts to friends; six, or possibly seven, copies are extant and details are given, in connection with each one, below. Variants are found, chiefly in the opening bars of the Waltz, as quoted here.

MSS. (1) Inscribed: 'à Mlle de Krudner, Paris, le 8 juin 1841': Conservatoire, Paris.

(2) Inscribed 'à Mme Oury, Paris, 10 decembre 1842':
    Dr Jacques Samuel, London.
(3) Fair copy, undated: Unknown.
(4) Undated, but with the title-page inscribed 'à
    Mlle Élise Gavard' (see **154**): Conservatoire, Paris.
(5) Fair copy: Delphine Potocka's album: 1844: see
    35.

(6) Fair copy, in another hand, but signed by Chopin:
    Bibliothèque de l'Opéra, Paris.
(7) Fair copy, possibly made by Fontana, and in all
    probability the source of Op. 70: no. 2: Con-
    servatoire, Paris.

(8) Fair copy: album of Anna Krüger, dated 8
    December, 1842. Public State Library, Leningrad.

139

TARANTELLA in A flat major, Op. 43. Summer 1841.

Publication:

Schuberth, Hamburg (449), December 1841.

Troupenas, Paris (1073), October 1841.

Wessel, London (5295), October 1841.

There is no dedication of Op. 43.

Since this work was paid for by Schuberth (500 fr.) on 1 July 1841, it is strange to read in a letter to Breitkopf & Haertel, of 29 July 1841, that the composer was still, apparently, negotiating with this firm for the publication of the Tarantella.

Wessel's edition was advertised in the *Musical World*, 28 October 1841. As an instance of the spurious dedications found in English editions of Chopin's works may be quoted that of a republication of Op. 43, by Augener, London: 'à mon [*sic*] ami Auguste Gathy'.

In a letter to Fontana, undated, but almost certainly of July 1841, Chopin wrote of the notation of the work and expressed the wish that it should be the same as Rossini's, in A major [*La Danza*].

MSS. (1) Fair copy: unknown. The MS. has a note in Chopin's hand with directions to Fontana to make three copies, writing out the repeats. None of the repeats in Chopin's MSS. are fully written out. The opus number on the title-page of this autograph was left blank.

  (2) Fair copy: Conservatoire, Paris. This MS. is one of Fontana's three copies; it is inscribed by a former owner: 'Ex Libris August Vinens, Parisis.'

140

MAZURKA in A minor (Émile Gaillard). 1840.

Publication:

M. Schlesinger, Paris. No. 1, in an *Album de Pianistes Polonais*, January 1841. The *Album* contained pieces by Chopin, Kontski, Klemezyński, Orda, Sowiński and Wolff. It was advertised in *A.M.Z.* for 20 January 1841, p. 72.

Republished by:

Jean Louis Chabal, Paris (erroneously as 'Op. 43'), Autumn 1841.

Bote & Bock, Berlin (3359), July 1855.

Dedicated to Émile Gaillard, a banker and pupil of Chopin's. The composer mentions him in a letter to Mlle Rozières, written on 3 September 1844.

The actual 'Op. 43' is the Tarantella in A flat (see previous item). On later issues, Chabal, a small music publisher in the Boulevard des Italiens, omitted this wrong number; one of these later issues was inscribed by Chopin for Jane Stirling.

MS. Lost.

140(B)

FOUR SONG FRAGMENTS. (?) 1840–7.

The manuscript of each song contains only the voice part. The manuscripts were with the firm of J. A. Stargardt, Marburg, at the dates shown in brackets.

(1) An eight-bar melody in A minor, 2/4. The manuscript is an autograph, but the heading 'Chopin. (paroles bohemes)' is in another hand. The words are coarse, and although they are in Polish, the orthography is German: e.g. *schla* for *szła*. (May 1970)

(2) A sixteen-bar melody, 2/4, headed 'F dur' (= F major). The text refers to the oppression of Poland by Russia and Prussia.

F   B.C.

Previously a Pole wore trousers, now his backside is
bare,
Because the Germans are robbing him and the
Muscovites oppress him.
Wait till the French come, they will cover our
backsides,
And to these rogues, the Prussians, for their crimes,
They will give such a hiding that the tufts of hair
will fly!

(February 1969)

(3) Sketch for a song in F minor, 2/4. There are twelve or
so bars. A similar melody is found in the 'Grand
Fantasia on Polish Airs', Op. 13 (**28**).

Oh, my man went to Danzig,
Oh, he will bring me some beads,
Oh, perhaps he is ill there....

(4) Sketches for a song in G major, 3/4. There are thirty
or so bars. No text is underlined but at the end of the
song Chopin has written the title 'Czulc serca'
('Tender Hearts'). The sketches for (3) and (4) are on
the same leaf; at the foot Kwiatkowski has written:
'Courlandic songs by T. Kwiatkowski, written down
by F. Chopin, Paris, 1847.' (February 1969)

141

PRELUDE in C sharp minor, Op. 45. August to September
1841.

Publication:

Pietro Mechetti, Vienna (3594), in a *Beethoven Album*, November 1841.

M. Schlesinger, Paris (3518), December 1841 (see note).

Wessel, London (5297), Ent. Sta. H. 20 January 1842.

Dedicated to Mlle la Princesse Elisabeth Czernicheff (see Chopin's letter to Fontana of October 1841 for his difficulties over the spelling of her name!).

Mechetti's *Beethoven Album* was in aid of the fund for the composer's monument at Bonn. It contained ten pieces, among them, besides Chopin's Prelude, Mendelssohn's 'Variations sérieuses', Op. 54. The C sharp minor Prelude was republished by Mechetti as a separate item – advertised in the *Wiener Zeitung* on 19 January 1842. On the title-page of this edition, the Viennese publisher gives Ewer, London, as the English publisher; this also may be the result of unsuccessful negotiations on Ewer's part for the publication of Chopin's works in England.

The composer wrote to Fontana on 1 October 1841: 'I have done the C sharp minor Prelude for Schlesinger.... Tomorrow I will send you a letter for Mechetti in which I will explain to him that if he wants a short thing for that "Album" I will give him today's Prelude.'

To Breitkopf & Haertel he wrote on 3 December 1841: 'Mechetti in Vienna has a Prelude for his "Beethoven" Album and a Polonaise' (see **135**).

Liszt edited this Prelude for the *Gesamtausgabe* of Breitkopf & Haertel, the only piece in the whole edition for which he was *de facto* responsible. A copy with revisions in several hands and with some remarks by Brahms is in the possession of Antony van Hoboken, Ascona.

The French edition first appeared in the first *Keepsake des Pianistes*, December 1841 (advertised in the *Revue et Gazette Musicale*) without publisher's number or dedication.

Wessel's edition was first advertised as *Prelude in E major*.

MS. Lost.

142

Two Nocturnes, Op. 48. October 1841.

No. 1 in C minor.
No. 2 in F sharp minor.

Publication:

> Breitkopf & Haertel, Leipzig (6653), January 1842 (advertised in December 1841).
> M. Schlesinger, Paris (3487–8), November 1841.
> Wessel, London (5300–1), Ent. Sta. H. 20 January 1842.

Dedicated to Mlle Laura Duperré, a daughter of Admiral Victor Guy Duperré (1775–1846), and a favourite pupil of Chopin's.

Chopin wrote to Fontana on 10 October 1841: 'Mme Sand's son will be in Paris about the 16th; I will send you by him the MSS. of the Concerto [Op. 46] and the Nocturnes [Op. 48].' To Breitkopf & Haertel (who paid for these Nocturnes by 13 December 1841) he wrote: 'I beg you to place on the title-page of my nocturnes, instead of Mlle Émilie, Mlle Laura Duperré.'

Wessel's edition called the first Nocturne 'Op. 48', the second 'Op. 48: *bis*'.

MS. State Collection, Warsaw (formerly with the Deutsche Staatsbibliothek). Both copies are in Fontana's hand, but the title-page of each one is in Chopin's hand, and a cover page for both bears in his hand the word: '13me et 14me Nocturnes pour piano forte dédiés à Mlle Laure Duperré.'

143

SONG for voice and PF., Op. 74: no. 8. 1841.

'Śliczny chłopiec' ('Wzniosły, smukły i młody')
'Handsome Lad' ('Strong, tall and young').
(D major)

German title: 'Mein Geliebter'.
Text: Bohdan Zaleski.

No. 8 Allegro moderato

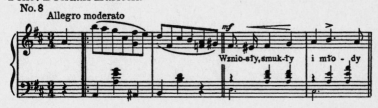

For details of the publication of Op. 74, see **32**.

MS. Lost.

144

FUGUE in A minor. 1841–2.

(Andante)

Publication:

Breitkopf & Haertel, Leipzig (Klavierbibliothek: 22,707), 1898.[1]

[1] This fugue is said to have been published in 1877, but I have been unable to ascertain any particulars of this publication.

(?) Metzler, Brussels, and (?) G. Schirmer, New York & London, 1898.

The work was announced by Breitkopf & Haertel as 'Fugue in A minor, for PF., by Fr. Chopin, revised and published according to the original manuscript in the possession of Natalie Janotha'. She introduced, in fact, unjustifiable changes in the text of the fugue. Chopin has made occasional alterations and revisions in the music itself; this seems to establish it as an original composition and not the copy of another's work.

There is a facsimile reproduction of the fugue in *Chybiński: Księga Pamiątkowa* ('Memorial Volume'), Cracow, 1950.

This A minor Fugue is not to be confused with the 'Cherubini' fugue mentioned by Niecks in his biography (English edition, vol. 1, p. 231). The four-page manuscript of a 'neat copy of one of Cherubini's fugues' said by Niecks to be in the possession of descendants of Franchomme, was offered for sale by Nicolas Rauch, Geneva, in November 1958. (A facsimile reproduction of one page is given in the sale catalogue, plate v.) It appears to consist of exercises based on subjects by Cherubini; the first page is headed by Chopin '2 Cherubini subjects' and the fourth page '3 countersubjects'.

MS. Museo de Chopin, La Cartuja, Valldemosa.

145

Three Mazurkas, Op. 50. Autumn 1841 to summer 1842.

No. 1 in G major.
No. 2 in A flat major.
No. 3 in C sharp minor.

Publication:

> Pietro Mechetti, Vienna (3682), (June) September 1842.
> M. Schlesinger, Paris (3692), (November 1842) spring 1843.
> Wessel, London (5303), (August) October 1842.

Dedicated to Leon Szmitkowski, a Polish compatriot in Paris; Chopin had referred to him in a letter of September 1833, as the 'slender Szmitkowski'. The English edition was dedicated by Wessel, without authorisation, to a 'Mr Field, of Bath'.

There is a possibility that the G major Mazurka was composed in 1841; Chopin wrote to Fontana on 1 October 1841 about a mazurka in Mechetti's possession 'already old'.

The dates in brackets above are of preliminary announcements. In the case of Mechetti's date there is confirmation in the Poznań journal *Literary Weekly*, but the actual publication date was probably September. Later advertisements of Schlesinger (*Gazette Musicale*) and Wessel (*Musical World*) withdrew the announcement. The final publication date in Paris is not known, but it was certainly early in 1843. Meanwhile the G major Mazurka was published alone by Schlesinger in the *Deuxième Keepsake des Pianistes*, November 1842. The *Keepsake* was an album of new pieces by Chopin,

Mendelssohn, Thalberg, etc., and was issued as a supplement for subscribers to the *Gazette Musicale*.

These facts suggest that Chopin failed to compose the second and third mazurkas in time for the publishers, for Schlesinger had prematurely announced the publication of Op. 50 as early as November 1841. They were not finished until the early summer of 1842 and are probably referred to in the composer's letter to Grzymała, undated, but of that period: 'Forgive me for asking you once more to send a letter to the Viennese publisher [Mechetti]...I ask the favour of you because it contains manuscripts of mine laboriously written out.'

MSS. (1) All three Mazurkas: Pierpont Morgan Library, New York.

    (2) No. 1, last part; MS. once in the possession of Émile Gaillard: Marc Loliée, Paris, *c.* 1953.

    (3) No. 3, in C sharp minor: Jagiellonian Library, Cracow. Presented by Dionizy Zaleski, from the collection of the poet Bohdan Zaleski, and a first, slightly shorter, version of the third Mazurka.

146

BALLADE no. 4, in F minor, Op. 52. 1842.

Publication:

> Breitkopf & Haertel, Leipzig (7001), November 1843.
> M. Schlesinger, Paris (3957), December 1843.
> Wessel, London (5305), (?) First advertised in April 1845.

Dedicated to Mme la Baronne Charlotte de Rothschild, wife of Nathaniel Rothschild. Chopin had been introduced to the family in 1832 by Prince Valentine Radziwill.

MSS. (1) Sketch consisting of the first 79 bars, differing from the printed version and inscribed 'pour Dessauer': Dr R. F. Kallir, New York. (For Dessauer, see **90**.)

(2) Final version: an album belonging to Mendelssohn's wife, Cécile and headed by Chopin 'Ballade, pour le piano, dédié à Madame la Baronne C. de Rothschild, par F. Chopin, Oeu. 52 ...': Bodleian Library, Oxford.

147

POLONAISE in A flat major, Op. 53. 1842.

Publication:

> Breitkopf & Haertel, Leipzig (7002), November 1843.
> M. Schlesinger, Paris (3958), December 1843.
> Wessel, London (5306), first advertised in April 1845.

Dedicated to Auguste Léo, Paris banker, patron of the arts, a relative of Moscheles.

For the supposed dedication to Clara Wieck, see **104**.

MSS. (1) Fragment, one passage consisting of bars 134–53: Robert Owen Lehman Foundation, Washington.

    (2) Complete MS: Heineman Foundation, New York (the copy originally owned by Clara Wieck, with Chopin's dedication to Léo).

148

SCHERZO no. 4, in E major, Op. 54. 1842.

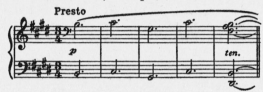

Publication:

    Breitkopf & Haertel, Leipzig (7003), November 1843.

    M. Schlesinger, Paris (3959), December 1843.

    Wessel, London (5307), first advertised in April 1845.

The German edition was dedicated to Mlle Jeanne de Caraman. The composer's decision to dedicate the French edition to Mlle Clothilde, the sister of Jeanne, was made too late to prevent the first printings of the title-page. This was then altered so clumsily that it had to be scrapped and the altered dedication required a new printing of the title-page.

Copies of the original page, clumsily altered, were with Arthur Hedley, London, and Antony van Hoboken, Ascona. The final title-page was reproduced in Bory's *Chopin: Vie par l'image*.

Jeanne and Clothilde de Caraman were both pupils of Chopin's.

MS. Jagiellonian Library, Cracow University. This MS. was originally used by Breitkopf & Haertel and contains Chopin's dedication to Jeanne de Caraman. (Formerly with Édouard Ganche.)

149

IMPROMPTU no. 3, in G flat major, Op. 51 ('Allegro Vivace'). Autumn 1842.

Publication:

> F. Hofmeister, Leipzig (2900), April 1843 (announced in February).
> M. Schlesinger, Paris (3847), July 1843.
> Wessel, London (5304), June 1843.

Dedicated to Mme la Comtesse Esterházy (*née* Joanne Batthyany), wife of Comte Alois Esterházy.

Chopin wrote to Breitkopf & Haertel on 15 December 1842: 'Besides these [Opp. 52, 53 and 54] I have written an Impromptu, of several pages, which I do not even offer to you, as I wish to oblige one of my old acquaintances, who for the last two years has been constantly asking me for something for Herr Hofmeister.' His letter assigning the Impromptu to Hofmeister and giving details of the dedication is dated 3 February 1843. He acknowledges the sum of 600 fr. from the publisher.

The work is called simply 'Allegro vivace' in the German edition.

The Impromptu appeared in Schlesinger's *La Revue et Gazette Musicale*, 9 July 1843, and was wrongly paginated. Chopin protested about this in a letter to the publisher of 22 July 1843. He asked for this correction to be published in the next issue:

> Page 3: *read* Page 5.
> Page 5: *read* Page 3.

MSS. (1) There is a first version of this Impromptu in the possession of the descendants of Chopin's young and gifted pupil Charles Filtsch. It may possibly be the version in F sharp major, referred to by the critic Maurice Bourges who, on 27 February 1842, wrote of a recital given by Chopin in Paris and mentioned an 'Impromptu in F sharp major'.

   (2) Fair copy: unknown, formerly in the Wilhelm Heyer Collection, Cologne. The autograph is headed simply 'Tempo giusto'.

150

WALTZ in A minor. (?) 1843.

Publication:

> *La Revue Musicale* (Editions Richard-Masse), Paris. Facsimile reproductions of the two MSS. are included and there is a foreword by Suzanne and Denise Chainaye, May 1955.

The Waltz was probably composed for Mme Charlotte de Rothschild, or her daughter. The MSS. were given to the Paris Conservatoire by a member of the Rothschild family in 1901.

J. G. Prod'homme, in the *Musical Quarterly*, New York, January 1939, referred to the waltz as 'a youthful work'. It was first described by the present writer in the *Monthly Musical Record*, March 1955, where the *incipit* was quoted to preclude any possible confusion with the A minor Waltz, Op. 34: no. 2.

MSS. (1) Rough draft.

(2) Fair copy entitled 'Walc'. Both manuscripts:
Conservatoire, Paris.

151

MODERATO in E major ('Albumblatt'). 1843.

Publication:

The periodical *Świat*, Warsaw, 4 June 1910, no. 23, p. 8,
edited by Henryk Pachulski.

Republished by:

Gebethner & Wolff, Warsaw, 1927, for the Warsaw
Committee collecting funds for the Chopin Monument (PN 5203).

Written in the album of Countess Anna Szeremetieff.
The piece is known as 'Albumblatt'. It has been called a
Prelude by Ferdinand Hoesick and a Nocturne by Zdzisłav
Jachimecki.

MS. Anna Szeremetieff's album, inscribed 'F. F. Chopin,
Paris, 1843': unknown.

152

TWO NOCTURNES, Op. 55. 1843.

No. 1 in F minor.
No. 2 in E flat minor.

Publication:

>   Breitkopf & Haertel, Leipzig (7142), August 1844.
>   M. Schlesinger, Paris (4084), August 1844.
>   Wessel, London (5308), first advertised in April 1845.

Dedicated to Jane Wilhelmina Stirling (1804–59), a younger daughter of John Stirling of Kippendavie and a pupil of Chopin's. A copy of the French edition with the dedication to Jane Stirling in the composer's hand is in the Jagiellonian Library, Cracow.

The contemporary handwritten copy of these nocturnes in this library may be in the hand of Fontana.

MSS. (1) No. 1, in F minor: Conservatoire, Paris.

>   (2) Nos. 1 and 2: Biblioteka Narodowa (National Library), Warsaw (with the dedication in the composer's hand).

>   (3) No. 1, in F minor. A sketch in F sharp minor, 16 bars long: album of Countess Elisabet de Cheremetieff, dated 'Paris, 8 Dec 1842': Central State Archives for Literature and Art, Moscow.

153

THREE MAZURKAS, Op. 56, 1843.

>   No. 1 in B major.
>   No. 2 in C major.
>   No. 3 in C minor.

Publication:

Breitkopf & Haertel, Leipzig (7143), August 1844.

M. Schlesinger, Paris (4085), August 1844.

Wessel, London (5309), first advertised April 1845.

Dedicated to Catherine Maberly, a friend of Jane Stirling and a pupil of Chopin's.

MSS. (1) No. 2, in C major, first sketch on one page: British Museum, London (formerly with Marcelline Czartoryska, then with E. H. W. Meyerstein).

(2) A second sketch for no. 2, in C major: unknown. This was reproduced in Kleczyński's *Chopin's Greater Works*, 1883, and shows Chopin's original penultimate bars to have consisted of a three-bar trill on a bass octave on the dominant. The MS. was again reproduced by Leichtentritt in 1905.

(3) The complete opus: Biblioteka Narodowa (National Library), Warsaw.

154

BERCEUSE in D flat major, Op. 57. 1843, revised in 1844.

Publication:

> Breitkopf & Haertel, Leipzig (7259) (May) July 1845.
> J. Meissonnier, Paris (2186), July 1845.
> Wessel, London (6313), June 1845.

Dedicated to Mlle Élise Gavard, a pupil of Chopin's. Her brother, Charles Gavard, was an acquaintance of the composer's in his last years and wrote reminiscences of him after his death. The dedication in Chopin's hand 'à Mlle Élise Gavard, son vieux professeur at ami, F. F. Chopin', on a separate page, is in the Paris Conservatoire.

The Berceuse was played by the composer on 2 February 1844 and revised at Nohant, the country residence of George Sand, later in the year. The journal *Gazette Musicale*, 5 January 1845, no. 1, p. 6, referred to the Sonata in B minor (see next) and the Berceuse when it reported Chopin's arrival in Paris from Nohant: 'Chopin est de retour à Paris; il rapporta une nouvelle grande sonate et des variantes. Bientôt ces deux importants ouvrages seront publiés.'

The term 'variantes' must have originated with the composer himself, and is justified by the MS. sketch in (1) below.

The Berceuse and the Sonata in B minor were published in Paris by Meissonnier and not Schlesinger, apparently because the latter wished to postpone publication against the composer's wishes (see his letters of 1 and 2 August 1844 to Franchomme).

Wessel's edition of the Berceuse is the only one in his complete series on which he printed the names of both continental publishers.

MSS. (1) First sketch, showing an embryonic 'variation' form: Robert Owen Lehman Foundation, Washington.

(2) Biblioteka Narodowa (National Library), Warsaw.

(3) Conservatoire, Paris. This 'definitive' text, as it has been called, still lacks the two introductory bars.

155

SONATA no. 2, in B minor, Op. 58, Summer 1844.

Publication:

Breitkopf & Haertel, Leipzig (7260), (May) July 1845.

J. Meissonnier, Paris (2187), July 1845.

Wessel, London (6314), June 1845.

Dedicated to Mme la Comtesse E. de Perthuis (see **89**); she is referred to as 'Perthuis' amiable wife'.

Brahms edited the Sonata for Breitkopf's *Gesamtausgabe* (vol. VIII).

There is an autograph copy of this Sonata made by Liszt, with his variant for the finale, in the Rocheblave Collection, Paris.

MSS. (1) Sketches: with the descendants of Franchomme.

       (2) Chopin Institute, Warsaw.

       (3) 1st movement, bars 33–5: Marc Loliée, Paris, *c.* 1953.

156

TWO SONGS for voice and PF., Op. 74: nos. 11 and 13. 1845.

No. 11. 'Dwojaki koniec' ('Rok się kochali...')
           'The Double End' ('They loved for a year...').

(D minor)

German Title: 'Zwei Leichen'.

No. 13. 'Nie ma czego trzeba' ('Mgła mi do oczu')
           'I want what I have not' ('Mist before my eyes')

(A minor)

German title: 'Melancolie'.

The texts of both songs are by Bohdan Zaleski.

For details of the publication of Op. 74, see **32**.

MSS. Lost.

157

THREE MAZURKAS, Op. 59. June to July 1845.

> No. 1 in A minor.
> No. 2 in A flat major.
> No. 3 in F sharp minor.

Publication:

> Stern, Berlin (71), November 1845.
> Brandus (successor to M. Schlesinger), Paris (4292), March 1846.
> Wessel, London (6315), December 1845.

There is no dedication of Op. 59.

Chopin wrote to his family on 20 July 1845: '...I have written three new mazurkas which will probably come out in Berlin, because a man I know has begged me for them: Stern, a good fellow and a learned musician, whose father is starting a music shop there.' Stern's business was purchased by Friedländer, Berlin, in 1852.

Schlesinger's business was acquired by Brandus early in 1846. The second of these mazurkas was given as a supplement to Schlesinger's *Revue et Gazette Musicale* on 24 May 1846, entitled: 'Mazurka nouvelle de Chopin'.

For Wessel's so-called 'Op. 59: *bis*', see **134**.

MSS. (1) No. 2, in A flat major: Bibliothèque de l'Opéra, Paris.

(2) No. 3, in F sharp minor: there is a first sketch for this Mazurka in G minor. The MS. was formerly in the Peters' Music Library. See *Jahrbuch der Musikbibliothek*, 1934: Pierpont Morgan Library, New York.

(3) No. 3, in F sharp minor: Mrs Eva Alberman, London. This copy, headed simply 'No. 3', was once owned by Hans von Bülow, together with the other two mazurkas of the opus. He gave no. 3 on 2 November 1864 to C. Kerfack from whom it passed first to the Wilhelm Meyer Collection, Cologne, and thence to its present owner.

(4) All three mazurkas: Boerner, Leipzig, 6 May 1911.

(5) Fair copy. Written in an album belonging to Mendelssohn's wife, Cécile, and inscribed by Chopin 'hommage à Madame F. Mendelssohn Bartholdy de la part de F. Chopin. Paris, 8 Oct 1845': Bodleian Library, Oxford.

158

BARCAROLLE in F sharp major, Op. 60. Autumn 1845 to summer 1846.

Publication:

> Breitkopf & Haertel, Leipzig (7545), November 1846.
> Brandus, Paris (4609), November 1846.
> Wessel, London (6317), September 1846.
>
> Dedicated to Mme la Baronne de Stockhausen (see **66**).

MSS. (1) Cracow University (former owner Baron de
Stockhausen, 1877; it passed to its present owners
from Édouard Ganche).

(2) Mrs Eva Alberman, London.

(3) Sketches: Chopin Institute, Warsaw.

159

POLONAISE-FANTAISIE in A flat major, Op. 61. Autumn
1845 to summer 1846.

Publication:

> Breitkopf & Haertel, Leipzig (7546), November 1846.
> Brandus, Paris (4610), November 1846.
> Wessel, London (6318), October 1846.

Dedicated to Mme A. Veyret, a mutual acquaintance of
Chopin and George Sand (see the composer's letter to
George Sand of 12 December 1847).

Chopin wrote to his family on 12 December 1845: '...I should like now to finish my violoncello sonata, barcarole and something else I don't know how to name...' – a reference to the Polonaise-Fantaisie.

Wessel's edition was on sale in London in October 1846.

MS. Sketches: Biblioteka Narodowa (National Library), Warsaw (originally with Breitkopf & Haertel).

160

SONATA in G minor, for PF. and cello, Op. 65. Autumn 1845–6.

Publication:

Breitkopf & Haertel, Leipzig (7718), January 1848.
Brandus, Paris (4744), October 1847.

Dedicated to Auguste Franchomme (1808–84), eminent French cellist and close friend of Chopin in the latter years of the composer's life.

Chopin wrote to his family on 11 October 1846: '. . . with my Sonata for cello I am now contented, now discontented.' He wrote again in April 1847: '. . . I played her [Delphine Potocka] my violoncello sonata with Franchomme, in my lodging.' (See also note to previous item.)

The Sonata was not published in England until the Paris Edition of Simon Richault (1860) (see Appendix III).

Breitkopf & Haertel announced the publication of the work in September 1847. Shortly after its actual publication, they published an arrangement for PF. and violin, by Ferdinand David.

Brandus, in the *Revue et Gazette Musicale*, 17 October 1847, advertised this work, together with Op. 63 and Op. 64, as 'to appear immediately'. The PF. Solo arrangement, published by Brandus, is by Moscheles.

MSS. (1) Sketch of the first movement: Conservatoire, Paris.

(2) One leaf of the first movement, and the Finale, headed 'Nohant, 1846': Mme Édouard André (a descendant of Franchomme).

(3) Fragmentary sketches for a (different?) Scherzo, seventeen bars: Biblioteka Narodowa (National Library), Warsaw.

(4) Twelve bars, signed and dated 'Paris, 23 May 1846': Besançon et Vincent, Paris, 23 March 1961.

(5) One leaf, containing 90 bars of a sketch for the scherzo: Stargardt, Marburg, June 1970.

160(B)

TWO BOURRÉES, written down by Chopin. (?) 1846.

No. 1 in G major.
No. 2 in A major.

Publication:

> Schott's, London (6708), July 1968 (together with the PF. arrangement of 'Wiosna', **117**, edited by Ateş Orga).

These airs were notated for the pianoforte and given a simple harmonisation by Chopin while he was at Nohant. They are supposed to be dance tunes native to Berry and were used by George Sand for the music in her play *François le Champi.*

MS. A music album of George Sand: Maurice Rheim, Paris, June 1957.

161

TWO NOCTURNES, Op. 62. 1846.

No. 1 in B major.
No. 2 in E major.

Publication:

> Breitkopf & Haertel, Leipzig (7547), November 1846.
> Brandus, Paris (4611), November 1846.
> Wessel, London (6319), October 1846.

Dedicated to Mlle R. de Könneritz, a pupil of Chopin's who later married Herr von Heygendorf. Copies of the pieces she studied with Chopin, corrected in his hand, were used as the basis of Peters' *Complete Edition* (1879). The dedication represents the composer's second thoughts: his first choice is vigorously scratched out from the MS. (2) below.

The second of these two nocturnes was republished in 1847 by *La Revue Musicale* in the 'Album des Pianistes', but without dedication or publisher's number.

MSS. (1) No. 1, in B major: Newberry Library, Chicago. It was originally with Brandus and contains the 'clean' dedication. It is reproduced in the 'Nocturnes' volume (VII) of the Polish 'Complete Edition'.

(2) No. 1, in B major: Biblioteka Narodowa (National Library), Warsaw (from the descendants of W. Grzymała). This MS. contains the cancelled dedication; it is reproduced in facsimile in Bory's *Chopin: Vie de l'image*.

(3) No. 2, in E major, formerly with the Brandus family: Museo de Chopin, La Cartuja, Valldemosa.

162

THREE MAZURKAS, Op. 63. Early autumn 1846.

> No. 1 in B major.
> No. 2 in F minor.
> No. 3 in C sharp minor.

Publication:

> Breitkopf & Haertel, Leipzig (7714), November 1847.
> Brandus, Paris (4742), October 1847.
> Wessel, London (no publisher's number printed), December 1847.

Dedicated to Mme la Comtesse Laura de Czosnowska.

Chopin referred to the composition of these three mazurkas in his letter to his family of 11 October 1846.

Breitkopf & Haertel announced publication on 8 September 1847.

Wessel's edition contained no publisher's number, but from the ones allotted to neighbouring opus numbers it should have been 6320. The three mazurkas were pirated by Cramer & Beale, London, who published them in June 1848.

On the French edition Jullien, London, is given as the English publisher [Louis Antoine Jullien]: this reveals further unsuccessful negotiations for the copyright of

Chopin's works in England, and shows the difficulties which Wessel was up against in his efforts to retain the right of being Chopin's sole publisher in England.

MSS. (1) No. 1, in B major: Conservatoire, Paris (at conclusion – 'Nohant, 1846').

(2) No. 2, in F minor, written in the album of René, Franchomme's little son: unknown.

163

MAZURKA in A minor, Op. 67 (Posth.): no. 4. 1846.

The mazurka exists in three versions:

Publication:

Version (*a*): For details of the publication of Op. 67, see **93**.

Version (*b*): *Dans le Souvenir de Frédéric Chopin*, Édouard Ganche, Paris, 1925, p. 236. This was the basis of the *Oxford Edition of Chopin's Works*, London, 1932, vol. III.

Version (*c*): Polish 'Complete Edition', 1956, vol. X, no. 47, *bis*: from MS. (3) below.

This is possibly a rejected mazurka from the collection for Op. 63 (previous item). The date is according to Fontana.

A copy of the mazurka, made by Thomas Tellefsen in May 1850 for Marcelline Czartoryska: unknown.

MSS. (1) Version (*a*): Lost.
     (2) Version (*b*): Unknown, formerly with Ganche.
     (3) Version (*c*): 'Gesellschaft der Musikfreunde', Vienna. It was originally in the possession of Brahms and is dated 'Paris, 48'.

164

THREE WALTZES, Op. 64. 1846–7.
    No. 1 in D flat major.
    No. 2 in C sharp minor.
    No. 3 in A flat major.

Publication:

    Breitkopf & Haertel, Leipzig (the three waltzes separately: 7715, 7716, 7717; the complete set: 7721), November 1847.

    Brandus, Paris (4743:1, 2 and 3), February 1848.

    Wessel, London (6321, 6322, 6323), September 1848.

Dedications in the French edition only:

No. 1, in D flat major: Countess Delphine Potocka (see 44).

No. 2, in C sharp minor: Baroness de Rothschild (see 146).

No. 3, in A flat major: Countess Catherine de Branicka, of the exiled Polish aristocracy in Paris, a pupil of Chopin's. Early editions gave this dedication to Baroness Bronicka.

Cramer & Beale's edition was pirated. They published the third Waltz later as 'Op. 64: no. 3'. The French edition again gave Jullien, London, as the English publisher (see 162).

Wessel may have published the complete opus after he had found that Cramer & Beale had published part of it; his publication of Op. 64 undoubtedly took place in September 1848: the acquisition date on the copy in the British Museum is 20 September 1848. It is clear from his publisher's numbers that the work was put into preparation at the same time as Op. 63.

The Waltz in D flat major is the so-called 'Minute' Waltz.

MSS. (1) Sketches: Royal College of Music, London.

(2) No. 1, in D flat major, two versions: Conservatoire, Paris.

(3) No. 2, in C sharp minor, first version: Conservatoire, Paris. This MS. was bequeathed to the Library of the Conservatoire by Baroness Charlotte de Rothschild. It was first published in the *Oxford Edition*, London, 1932, vol. 1. In this version, the upbeat on the third crotchet of the first bar is omitted by Chopin.

(4) No. 2 and No. 3, in A flat major, first sketches: Bibliothèque de l'Opéra, Paris. (The second originally with Marcelline Czartoryska.)

165

SONG for voice and PF., Op. 74: no. 9. 1847.

'Melodya' ('Z gór, gdźie dzwigali strasznych krzyżów')
'Melody' ('From the mountains they bore the terrible
crosses').

(G major/E minor)

German title: 'Eine Melodie'.
Text: Zygmunt Krasiński. (Early editions of the song give
'Author unknown'.)

For details of the publication of Op. 74, see **32**.

MS. Delphine Potocka's album: below his signature
Chopin is said to have written the celebrated lines
from Dante's *Inferno*, canto v, 121:

> Nessun maggiore dolore
> Che ricordarsi del tempo felice
> Nella miseria.

166

WALTZ in B major. 12 October 1848.

Unpublished

The Waltz was written for Mrs Erskine, Jane Stirling's
elder sister. It was discovered in 1952 by Arthur Hedley.

MS. Unknown.

167

MAZURKA in G minor, Op. 67 (Posth.): no. 2. Summer 1849.

For details of the publication of Op. 67, see **93**.

In Louise's list this mazurka is dated '1848'.

MS. Lost.

168

MAZURKA in F minor, Op. 68 (Posth.): no. 4. Summer 1849.

For details of the publication of Op. 68, see **18** and also note below.

In Louise's list this Mazurka is dated '1848'. According to Fontana this is Chopin's last composition, but it is not the final version from Chopin's pen, being, in fact, a mazurka 'realised' by August Franchomme from Chopin's sketches, in June 1852 (see *Souvenirs inédits de Chopin*, p. 196). Arthur Hedley discovered the original MS. version in the papers of the Lemire-André family, descendants of Franchomme. It contains an episode in F major, omitted by Franchomme in his 'realisation'.

A. M. Schlesinger published the piece separately in 1852, as the *Dernière Pensée Mazurka*, that is, three years before Fontana's publication of Op. 68.

The Mazurka was published in a fuller version by Jan Ekier: 'Polskie Wydawnictwo Muzyczne' (5817), 1965. This edition contains a facsimile of Chopin's manuscript, together with a facsimile of Franchomme's version used by Fontana in 1855.

MS. First draft (formerly with the Lemire-André family): Biblioteka Narodowa (National Library), Warsaw.

168(B)

SONG for voice and PF. Date unknown.

'Patryot Piesn' ('Patriotic Song').

Text: S. Hernisz.

Publication:
J. K. Zupanski, Poznan, 1960.

MS. Kórnik Library.

APPENDIXES

Appendix I

CHRONOLOGICAL SEQUENCE OF PUBLICATION

1817
.... Military March (lost)
November Polonaise in G minor (republ. 1927)

1825
June Rondo, Op. 1

1826
.... Mazurkas in B flat and G (2nd versions: republ. 1851)
Polonaise in B flat minor (republ. 1879)

1828
February Rondo à la Mazur, Op. 5

1830
January Variations for PF. and Orch., Op. 2

1831
Autumn Introduction and Polonaise, Op. 3

1832
December PF. Trio in G minor, Op. 8
3 Nocturnes, Op. 9
4 Mazurkas, Op. 6
5 Mazurkas, Op. 7

1833
July Études, Op. 10
PF. Concerto, Op. 11
Grand Duo (*Robert le Diable*)
November Variations (*Ludovic*), Op. 12
December 3 Nocturnes, Op. 15

1834

March	Introduction and Rondo, Op. 16
	4 Mazurkas, Op. 17
April	Fantaisie on Polish Airs, Op. 13
June	Waltz, Op. 18
July	Rondo, 'Krakowiak', Op. 14
October	Bolero, Op. 19

1835

| February | Scherzo, Op. 20 |

1836

January	4 Mazurkas, Op. 24
April	PF. Concerto, Op. 21
May	2 Nocturnes, Op. 27
June	Ballade, Op. 23
July	2 Polonaises, Op. 26
August	*Andante spianato* and Polonaise, Op. 22
....	2 Songs ('Zycenie' and 'Wojak'), publ. anonymously

1837

October	Études, Op. 25
December	4 Mazurkas, Op. 30
	Scherzo, Op. 31
	2 Nocturnes, Op. 32

1838

| October | 4 Mazurkas, Op. 33 |
| December | 3 Waltzes, Op. 34 |

1839

| June | *Hexameron*, Variation in E major |
| | Preludes, Op. 28 |

1840

May	Sonata, Op. 35
	Impromptu, Op. 36
June	2 Nocturnes, Op. 37
	Waltz in A flat, Op. 42
September	Ballade, Op. 38
October	Scherzo, Op. 39
November	Trois Nouvelles Études

December   2 Polonaises, Op. 40
              4 Mazurkas, Op. 41

1841

October   Mazurka in A minor (Émile Gaillard)
              Tarantella, Op. 43
November   Polonaise, Op. 44
              Prelude, Op. 45
              Allegro de Concert, Op. 46
              Ballade, Op. 47
              2 Nocturnes, Op. 48
              Fantasia in F minor, Op. 49

1842

February   Mazurka in A minor (*Notre Temps*)
September 3 Mazurkas, Op. 50

1843

April   Impromptu, Op. 51
November   Ballade, Op. 52
              Polonaise, Op. 53
              Scherzo, Op. 54

1844

August   2 Nocturnes, Op. 55
              3 Mazurkas, Op. 56

1845

June   Berceuse, Op. 57
              Sonata, Op. 58
November   3 Mazurkas, Op. 59

1846

October   Barcarolle, Op. 60
              Polonaise-Fantaisie, Op. 61
              2 Nocturnes, Op. 62

1847

October   3 Mazurkas, Op. 63
              3 Waltzes, Op. 64
              Sonata for PF. and cello, Op. 65.

                                         B.C.

Posthumous publication:

1851

May   'Schwiezerbub' Variations
           Sonata, Op. 4

1852

....   Deux valses mélancoliques (Op. 70: no. 2; Op. 69: no. 2)

1855

May   Fantaisie-Impromptu, Op. 66
           4 Mazurkas, Op. 67
           4 Mazurkas, Op. 68
           2 Waltzes, Op. 69
           3 Waltzes, Op. 70
           3 Polonaises, Op. 71
           Nocturne, Funeral March, 3 Écossaises, Op. 72
           Rondo for two pianofortes, Op. 73

1856

....   2 songs republ. from 1836, with Chopin's name

1857

....   16 Polish songs, Op. 74

1859–60

....   16 songs with German translations

1864

....   Polonaise in G sharp minor

1868

....   Waltz in E minor

1870

....   Polonaise in G flat major
           Mazurka in C major
           Song ('Polens Grabgesang'), Op. 74: no. 17

1871

....   Waltz in E major

1875

January   Nocturne (*Lento con gran espressione*)
Mazurka in D major (1st version)
Mazurkas in B flat and G major (1st versions)

1879

....   Mazurka in G ('Prague')

1880

January   Mazurka in D major (2nd version)

1881

....   Variations in A major (on a theme by Paganini)

1898

....   Fugue in A minor

1902

....   Polonaise in A flat (corrupt: 'clean' in 1908)
Waltz in A flat
Waltz in E flat
Mazurka in A minor (1st version, Op. 7: no. 2)

1909

....   Mazurka in B flat (A. Wolowska)

1910

February   Mazurka ('Mazurek') in D major
Song: 'Czary'
June   Moderato in E major (republ. 1827)
October   Song: 'Dumka'

1918

August   Prelude in A flat (Pierre Wolff)

1930

....   Mazurka in A flat (Céline Szymanowska)

1931

....   Cantabile in B flat major

1934

....   Contredanse in G flat major
Polonaise in B flat major (republ. 1937)

1938
.... Nocturne in C minor
Largo in E flat

1954
.... Rondo (1st version of Op. 73)

1955
May   Waltz in A minor
Waltz in E flat

1965
.... Mazurka in F minor, Op. 68: no. 4 ('clean')
Variations in D major, for PF. duet

1968
.... 'Wiosna', arr. for PF. solo
2 Bourrées

Appendix II

PUBLISHERS OF THE FIRST EDITIONS

A. ENGLAND

London   Wessel & Co.: Opp. 1–3, 5–11, 13–64; *Notre Temps* Mazurka;
'Deux valses mélancoliques'; 'Émile Gaillard' Mazurka
Cocks.: Op. 4; 'Schweizerbub' Variations
Cramer, Addison & Beale: Op. 12; *Hexameron* Variation
Francis, Day & Hunter; Waltz in E flat
Stanley Lucas, Weber & Co.: Op.74.

B. FRANCE

Paris   Maurice Schlesinger: Opp. 1, 2, 6–18, 20–7, 29–34, 44–56;
'Grand Duo'; Trois Nouvelles Études
Brandus (successor to Schlesinger): Opp. 59–65
Eugène Troupenas: Opp. 35–41, 43; *Notre Temps* Mazurka
Joseph Meissonnier: Opp. 57, 58
Joseph Meissonnier Fils: Opp. 66–73
Adolph Catalan et Cie: Op. 28
A. F. G. Pacini: Op. 42
Prillip et Cie: Op. 19
Simon Richault: Opp. 3, 4; 'Schweizerbub' Variations
Schoenenberger: Op. 5
Chabal: 'Émile Gaillard' Mazurka
Revue Musicale: Waltz in A minor
J. Hamelle: Op. 74

C. GERMANY AND AUSTRIA

Leipzig   Breitkopf & Haertel: Opp. 12, 15–18, 20–31, 33–42, 46–9,
52–8, 60–5; Waltzes in A flat and E flat; Mazurka in D
major (two versions)
Kistner: Opp. 6–11, 13, 14
Peters: Op. 19
Hofmeister: Opp. 5, 51
Mainz   B. Schotts Sons: Polonaises in G sharp minor and G flat;
Notre Temps Mazurka; Mazurka in C; Waltz in E minor

Berlin   A. M. Schlesinger: Opp. 1, 32, 66–74; 'Grand Duo'; Trois
Nouvelles Études.
Stern & Co.: Op. 59
Bote & Bock: 'Émile Gaillard' Mazurka
Hamburg Schuberth & Co.: Op. 43
Vienna   Tobias Haslinger: Op. 2; 'Schweizerbub' Variations
Pietro Mechetti: Opp. 3, 44, 45, 50

D. POLAND

Cracow   W. Chaberski: Waltz in E minor
J. Wildt: Deux valses mélancoliques
Krzyanówski, S. A.: Polonaises in A flat and B flat
Lwow   *Lamus*, 1909: Mazurka in B flat
Poznań   J. Leitgeber: 'Lento con gran espressione'; Mazurka in D
major (1st version)
Warsaw   J. J. Cybulski: Polonaise in G minor
Andrea Brzezina & Co.: Opp. 1, 5
R. Friedlein: Mazurkas in B flat and G major
Gebethner & Wolff: Mazurka in A flat; Op. 74; *Moderato*
in E major
J. Kauffmann: Waltz in E minor; Mazurka in C major;
Polonaises in G sharp minor and G flat
Echo Muzyczne, 1881: Variations on a theme by Paganini
Muzyka, 1931: Cantabile in B flat major

E. SWITZERLAND

Geneva   *Pages d'Art*, 1918: Prelude in A flat major

Appendix III

COMPLETE EDITIONS

The following list is selective; only those complete editions with some claim to have been based on original material have been included. The order is chronological.

1. Wessel & Co., London, *c.* 1853

'Wessel & Co. Complete Collection of the Compositions of Frederic Chopin for the Piano-Forte.' (For the 71 items in this collection, see Appendix IV.)

The first and most complete of the nineteenth-century editions prior to that of Breitkopf & Haertel, 1878–80.

2. Simon Richault, Paris, *c.* 1860

'New and cheap Paris edition. The Works of Frédéric Chopin.' Edited by Thomas Tellefsen. 12 volumes, excluding the songs.

Tellefsen (1823–74) was a pupil of Chopin's for a short time.

[Schoenenberger, Paris, 1860. Vols 21–24 of the publisher's 'Bibliothèque Classique des Pianistes' were devoted to the PF. works of Chopin. They were called 'Œuvres Complètes' and were supplied with a biography and analyses by Fétis, but it was not, in fact, a complete collection.]

3. Gebethner, Warsaw, 1863

'Frédéric Chopin; œuvres pour le piano, édition originale; Varsovie, 1863.'

The edition was authorised by the composer's family. There were no songs. It was revised in 1877 and published in six volumes by the firm, then Gebethner & Wolff. It contained all the opus numbers up to Op. 73, with the exception of Op. 65, and it was arranged numerically, by opus numbers. The songs were added in 1880.

A third edition, edited by Jan Kleczeński and containing various supplementary works, was published in 1882, in ten volumes.

4. P. Jurgenson, Moscow, 1873–6

'Complete Works of Chopin, critically revised after the original French, German and Polish editions by Karl Klindworth.' The edition contains PF. works only, and was in six volumes.

Klindworth (1830–1916) was a pupil of Liszt.

5. Breitkopf & Haertel, Leipzig, 1878–80

'First critically revised complete edition, edited by Woldemar Bargiel, Johannes Brahms, Auguste Franchomme, Franz Liszt, Carl Reinecke, Ernst Rudorff.'

The songs were translated by Hans Schmidt. This was the most complete edition to date, and contained 213 items in 14 volumes. It replaced a slightly earlier, but inferior, 'complete' edition by this firm, edited by Carl Reinecke and called *Neue Revidirte Ausgabe*, in ten volumes.

A supplement, containing the Waltzes in A flat and E flat, and the first version of the A minor Mazurka, Op. 7: no. 2, was added in 1902.

6. F. Kistner, Leipzig, 1879

'Fréd. Chopin's Works, revised and fingered (for the most part according to the composer's notes) by Karl Mikuli.' 17 volumes.

Mikuli (1821–88) was a pupil of Chopin's from 1844 to 1848; he was assisted in preparing this edition by his fellow-pupil Friederike Müller-Streicher.

7. C. F. Peters, Leipzig, 1879

'Fr. Chopin's Collected Works.' 12 volumes.

This was edited by Hermann Scholtz (d. 1918). He used the autographs of Op. 7: no. 3, Opp. 28, 48, 51 and 54, and a sketch of Op. 30: no. 4. He also used various printed editions which had been corrected by Chopin for his pupils Frau von Heygendorf and Georg Mathias.

8. Oxford University Press, London, 1932

The Oxford Original Edition of Fr. Chopin. Edited by Édouard Ganche, Président de la Société Fr. Chopin, à Paris. 3 volumes, PF. Works only.

The edition was based on original French editions belonging to Jane Stirling, corrected in Chopin's hand. They went to Ganche from Mrs Anne D. Houston, a great-niece of Jane Stirling's. There are prefaces in English, French and German.

9. Polish Complete Edition, Warsaw, 1937–

'Complete Works of Frederick Chopin' ('Dzieła Wszystkie Fryderyk Chopina'), edited by Ignacy Paderewski, Ludwik Bronarski and Josef Turczyński. 26 volumes.

The edition is based on original MSS. and first editions, with a supplementary 'Editors' Report' to each volume. The project was inspired in 1937 by the Frédéric Chopin Institute of Warsaw and the Polish Music Publishers' Association of Cracow.

The last eight volumes are to consist of full scores and parts. There are prefaces in Polish to all volumes, and English, French and Russian editions of these are gradually appearing.

Appendix IV

WESSEL'S COMPLETE EDITION

Nº			
1.	'Adieu à Varsovie' *Rondeau*	Op.	1
2.	'Homage [*sic*] à Mozart' *Grandes Var. brill.* on 'LA CI DAREM' *from Don Giovanni*	Op.	2
3.	'La Gaieté' *Intr. et Polonaise brillante*	Op.	3
4.	'La Posiana' *Rondeau à la Mazur*	Op.	5
5.	'Souvenir de la Pologne' 1st set of Mazurkas	Op.	6
6.	2nd set of Mazurkas	Op.	7
7.	'Murmures de la Seine' 1st set of Nocturnes	Op.	9
8.	2nd set of Nocturnes	Op.	9

[Op. 8 had been published by Wessel, although he did not include it in the Complete Edition.]

9.	'Douze Grandes Études' Bk. 1	Op.	10
10.	Bk. 2	Op.	10
XI. [*sic*]	'First Grand Concerto'	Op.	11
12.	'Fantasie brillante' *sur des airs nationaux polonois*	Op.	13
13.	'Krakovia' *Grand Rondeau de Concert*	Op.	14
14.	'Les Zephyrs', 3rd set of Notturnos	Op.	15
15.	'Rondo Élégante'	Op.	16
16.	'Souvenirs de la Pologne' 3rd set of Mazurkas	Op.	17
17.	'Invitation pour la danse' *Grand Valse*	Op.	18
18.	'Souvenir d'Andalousie' *Bolero*	Op.	19
19.	'Le Banquet infernal' 1st Scherzo	Op.	20
20.	'Second Grand Concerto'	Op.	21
21.	'Grand polonoise brillante' *précédée d'un Andante spianato*	Op.	22
22.	'La Favorite' *Ballade (ohne Worte)*	Op.	23
23.	'Souvenir de la Pologne' 4th set of Mazurkas	Op.	24
24.	'Douze Études' 3rd set of Studies	Op.	25
25.	Idem 4th set of Studies	Op.	25
26.	'Les Favorites' *Deux Polonoises*	Op.	26
27.	'Les Plaintives' 4th set of Notturnos	Op.	27
28.	'Twenty-four Grand Preludes' *through all keys* 5th set of Studies	Op.	28
29.	6th set of Studies	Op.	28

30.	'First Impromptu'		Op. 29
31.	'Souvenir de Pologne'	5th set of Mazurkas	Op. 30
32.	'Second Scherzo'		Op. 31
33.	'Il Lamento e la Consolazione' 5th set of Notturnos		Op. 32
34.	'Souvenir de la Pologne'	6th set of Mazurkas.	Op. 33
35.	'Trois Grandes Valses'	Bk. 1	Op. 34
36.		Bk. 2	Op. 34
37.		Bk. 3	Op. 34
38.	'Grande Sonate'		Op. 35
39.	'Second Impromptu'		Op. 36
40.	'Les Soupirs'	6th set of Notturnos	Op. 37
41.	'La Gracieuse' *2de Ballade* (*ohne Worte*)		Op. 38
42.	'Third Scherzo'		Op. 39
43.	'Les Favorites'	*Deux Polonoises* (Set 2)	Op. 40
44.	'Souvenir de la Pologne'	7th set of Mazurkas	Op. 41
45.	'Grande Valse'		Op. 42
46.	'Tarantelle'		Op. 43
47.	'Grande Polonoise'		Op. 44
48.	'Prelude' (in E [*sic*])		Op. 45
49.	'Allegro *de* concert'		Op. 46
50.	'Third Ballade'		Op. 47
51.	'Thirteenth Nocturne'		Op. 48
52.	'Fourteenth Nocturne'		Op. 48
53.	'Grand Fantasia'		Op. 49
54.	'Souvenir de la Pologne'	8th set of Mazurkas	Op. 50
55.	'Third Impromptu'		Op. 51
56.	'Fourth Ballade'		Op. 52
57.	'Eighth Polonaise'		Op. 53
58.	'Fourth Scherzo'		Op. 54
59.	'15ᵐᵉ & 16ᵐᵉ Nocturno'		Op. 55
60.	'Souvenir de la Pologne'	9th set of Mazurkas	Op. 56
61.	'La Berceuse' *Andante*		Op. 57
62.	'Second Grande Sonate'		Op. 58
63.	'Souvenirs de la Pologne'	10th set of Mazurkas	Op. 59
64.	'Cracow' Mazurka		Op. 59: *bis*
65.	'Barcarolle'		Op. 60
66.	'Polonaise Fantaisie'		Op. 61
67.	'17ᵐᵉ & 18ᵐᵉ Nocturno'		Op. 62
68.	'Souvenirs de la Pologne'	11th set of Mazurkas	Op. 63
69.	'Deux Valses'	N° 1	
70.	D°	N° 2	Op. 64
71.	'Valse'	N° 3	

Appendix V

DEDICATIONS

Agoult, Marie, Comtesse d'	- 12 Studies, Op. 25
Albrecht, Thomas - -	- Scherzo, Op. 20
Apponyi, Comtesse d' -	- 2 Nocturnes, Op. 27
Beauvau, Princesse Ludmilla de	- Polonaise, Op. 44
Belgiojoso, Princesse Christine de	*Hexameron* variation in E major
Billing, Baronne de - -	- 2 Nocturnes, Op. 32
Branicka, Comtesse Catherine de	Waltz, Op. 64: no. 3
Caraman, Clothide de - -	- Scherzo, Op. 54 (French edition)
Caraman, Jeanne de - -	- Scherzo, Op. 54 (German edition)
Czartoryska, Princess Adam	- 'Krakowiak' Rondo, Op. 14
Czernicheff, Princess Elisabeth	- Prelude, Op. 45
Czosnowska, Countess Laura de	- 3 Mazurkas, Op. 63
Dessauer, Josef - - -	- 2 Polonaises, Op. 26
Duperre, Mlle Laura - -	- 2 Nocturnes, Op. 48
Dupont, Mme (? Sofie) -	- Polonaise in G sharp minor
Eichtal, Mlle A. d' - -	- Waltz, Op. 34: no. 3
Elsner, Emily - - -	- Waltzes in A flat and E flat; Mazurka, Op. 7: no. 2 (1st version)
Elsner, Josef - - -	- Sonata, Op. 4 (Posth.)
Est, Baronne d' - - -	- Polonaise, Op. 22
Esté, Mme d' - - -	- Fantaisie-Impromptu, Op. 66 (Posth.)
Esterházy, Comtesse - -	- Impromptu, Op. 51
Flahault, Comtesse Émilie de	- Bolero, Op. 19
Fontana, Julian - - -	- 2 Polonaises, Op. 40
Franchomme, Auguste -	- Sonata for PF. and cello, Op. 65
Freppa, Mme Lina - -	- 4 Mazurkas, Op. 17
Fürstenstein, Comtesse Adèle de	- Scherzo, Op. 31
Gaillard, Émile - - -	- Mazurka in A minor; Waltz in E flat
Gavard, Élise - - -	- Berceuse, Op. 57
Gladowska, Konstancja -	- Waltz, Op. 70: no. 3
Gutman, Adolf - - -	- Scherzo, Op. 39

Hanka, Vaclav - - -	- Mazurka in G major
Hartmann, Caroline - -	- Rondo, Op. 16
Hiller, Ferdinand - -	- 3 Nocturnes, Op. 15
Hoffmann, Klementyna -	- Mazurka, Op. 67: no. 3
Horsford, Emma - -	- *Ludovic* Variations, Op. 12
Horsford, Laura - - -	- Waltz, Op. 18
Ivri, Baronne C.d' - -	- Waltz, Op. 34: no. 2
Jędrzejewicz, Louise (*née* Chopin)	*Lento con gran espressione*
Johns, Paul Émile - -	- 5 Mazurkas, Op. 7
Kalkbrenner, Friedrich -	- Concerto, Op. 11
Kessler, Joseph Christoph -	- Preludes, Op. 28 (German edition)
Kolberg, Wilhelm - -	- Mazurka, Op. 7: no. 4; Polonaise in B flat minor
Könneritz, Mlle R. de -	- 2 Nocturnes, Op. 62
Léo, Auguste - - -	- Polonaise, Op. 53
Linde, Mme - - -	- Rondo, Op. 1
Liszt, Franz - - -	- Studies, Op. 10
Lobau, Comtesse Caroline de	- Impromptu, Op. 29
Maberly, Catherine - -	- 3 Mazurkas, Op. 56
Merk, Josef - - -	- Polonaise, Op. 3
Mlokosiewicz, Mlle - -	- Mazurka, Op. 67: no. 1
Moriolles, Comtesse A. de -	- Rondo à la Mazur, Op. 5
Mostowska, Comtesse Rosa	- 4 Mazurkas, Op. 33
Müller, Friederike - -	- 'Allegro de Concert', Op. 46
Noailles, Pauline de - -	- Ballade, Op. 47
Perthuis, Comte de - -	- 4 Mazurkas, Op. 24
Perthuis, Comtesse de - -	- Sonata, Op. 58
Pixis, Johann Peter - -	- Fantaisie on Polish Airs, Op. 13
Plater, Comtesse Pauline -	- 4 Mazurkas, Op. 6
Pleyel, Cammille - - -	- Preludes, Op. 28 (French edition)
Pleyel, Marie - - -	- 3 Nocturnes, Op. 9
Potocka, Comtesse Delphine	- Concerto, Op. 21; Waltz, Op. 64: no. 1
Radziwill, Prince Antoine -	- PF. Trio, Op. 8
Rothschild, Baronne C. de -	- Ballade, Op. 52; Waltz, Op. 64: no.2
Schumann, Robert - -	- Ballade, Op. 38
Skarbek, Comte Michel -	- Polonaise, Op. 71: no. 1
Skarbek, Wiktoria - -	- Polonaise in G minor
Souzzo, Princesse Catherine de	- Fantaisie, Op. 49
Sowińska, Katarzyna - -	- 'Schweizerbub' Variations
Stirling, Jane - - -	- 2 Nocturnes, Op. 55
Stockhausen, Baron de -	- Ballade, Op. 23
Stockhausen, Baronne de -	- Barcarolle, Op. 60
Szeremetieff, Anna - -	- *Moderato* in E major

Szmitkowski, Leon - -	- 3 Mazurkas, Op. 50
Szymanowska, Celina - -	- Mazurka in A flat
Thun-Hohenstein, Mlle de -	- Waltz, Op. 34: no. 1
Veyret, Mme A. - - -	- Polonaise-Fantaisie, Op. 61
Witwicki, Stefan - - -	- 4 Mazurkas, Op. 41
Wodzińska, Maria - -	- Waltz, Op. 69: no. 1
Wolff, Pierre - - -	- Prelude in A flat
Wolowska, Alexandra - -	- Mazurka in B flat
Woyciechowski, Titus -	- Variations, PF. Duet; Variations, Op. 2 [Chopin intended Op. 40: no. 1 to be dedicated to Woyciechowski]
Württemberg, Princesse de -	- 4 Mazurkas, Op. 30
Żwyny, Wojciech - -	- Polonaise in A flat

Appendix VI

THE POETS OF CHOPIN'S SONGS

1. Count Zygmunt Krasiński (1812–59): poet of mystic patriotism and friend of Mickiewicz. His poems include the 'Undivine Comedy', the 'Psalm of Life' and the drama *Irydion*.
    Author of the song 'Melodya' (**165**).

2. Adam Bernard Mickiewicz (1798–1855): Poland's greatest poet-patriot. Author of *The Ancestors, Crimean Sonnets, Konrad Wallenrod* and of the poem 'Świteź' on which Chopin's Ballade (Op. 38) is supposed to be based. In July 1834 Mickiewicz married Celina Szymanowska, daughter of Maria Szymanowska. He resided intermittently in Paris from 1832 onwards. He was at one time Professeur au Collège de France, and became acquainted with Chopin, who played the piano at his home *c.* 1835.
    Author of the songs: 'Precz z moich oczu!' (**48**),
    'Moja piesz czotka' (**112**).

3. Wincenty Pol (1809–76): a soldier-poet and patriot. His chief poem is 'The Song of our Land' – a description in verse of districts in Poland.
    Author of the song: 'Śpiew grobowy' (**101**)

4. Stefan Witwicki (1800–47): a lyric poet but a minor figure in Polish literature. A friend of Mickiewicz in Paris for a short time, but the two quarrelled over political matters. Witwicki enjoyed a closer acquaintance with Chopin than any other of the associated poets. He died of a spinal disease in Rome.
    Author of the songs:

'Życenie' (**33**)	'Czary' (**51**)
'Gdzie lubi' (**32**)	'Smutna Rzeka' (**63**)
'Wojak' (**47**)	'Narzeczony' (**63**)
'Hulanka' (**50**)	'Pierscien' (**103**)
'Posel' (**50**)	'Wiosna' (**116**)

5. Josef Bohdan Zaleski (1802–86): called the Ukrainian Nightingale by Mickiewicz, with whom he enjoyed a close friendship in Paris in the 1830s. His poetry has the 'wild charm, the mystic music of the Steppes'. His most famous poem is called 'The Spirit of the Steppe'.

Author of the songs:

'Śliczny chłopiec' (**143**)	'Dwojaki koniec' (**156**)
'Dumka' (**132**)	'Nie ma czego trzeba' (**156**)

6. Ludwik Osiński (1775–1838): poet, critic and the main representative of Polish pseudo-classicism.
   Author of the song: 'Piosna litewska' (**63**).

Appendix VII

CHOPIN'S ADDRESSES IN PARIS

August 1831 to end of 1832:	Boulevard Poissonnière 27
1833:	Cité Bergère 4
End of 1833 to September 1836:	Rue de Montblanc 5 ⎱ Rue de la Chaussée d'Anton ⎰ The same house with a double address.
October 1836 to November 1838:	Rue de la Chaussée d'Anton 38
[Majorca]	
October 1839 to summer 1841:	Rue Tronchet 5
October 1841 to October 1842:	Rue Pigalle 16
October 1842 to June 1849:	Cité d'Orléans Place d'Orléans 9 ⎱ Rue St Lazare 34 ⎰ The same house, with a double address.
June 1849 to September 1849:	Grande rue 74, Chaillot
September 1849 to October 1849:	Place Vendôme 12

Appendix VIII

THREE AUTOGRAPH ALBUMS

1. Emily Elsner (before 1830):
   Waltz in A flat (21), Waltz in E flat (46), Mazurka, Op. 7: no. 2 (45); seven songs: 'Gdzie lubi' (32), 'Życzenie' (33), 'Wojak' (47), 'Precz z moich oczu!' (48), 'Hulanka' (50), 'Posel' (50), 'Czary' (51).
   Part of this album was destroyed in the Second World War; the rest is in the possession of the Society of Music, Warsaw.

2. Maria Wodzińska (1836):
   Nocturne: *Lento con gran espressione*, in C sharp minor (49); Seven songs: 'Gdzie lubi', 'Wojak', 'Precz z moich oczu!', 'Hulanka', 'Posel', 'Czary', 'Piosnka litewska' (63).
   This album, for over fifty years accepted as in Chopin's own handwriting, is now believed to be in the hand of his sister, Louise. It was intended by Chopin to be a kind of love-token to Maria and the fact that he asked his sister to write out the contents of it throws an interesting light on, first, his relationship with Maria, and second, on his well-known dislike of writing out music. The album is part of the State Collection, Warsaw.

3. Delphine Potocka (1836–44):
   Prelude in A major, Op. 28: no. 7 (100);
   Two waltzes, published as 'Deux valses mélancoliques'
   (*a*) in B minor (35)
   (*b*) in F minor (138)
   Song: 'Melodya' (165).
   This album, whose whereabouts is unknown, contained a Mazurka in F sharp major, which Chopin had presumably copied out for Delphine, without adding the composer's name. As a result, the Viennese publisher, J. P. Gotthard, published the work in good faith, 1873, as a Mazurka by Chopin. The mis-attribution was pointed out soon afterwards by Ernst Pauer who gave, at the same time, the rightful author's name – Charles Mayer.

Appendix IX

BIBLIOGRAPHY

Polish subtitles are translated in brackets

Journal of the Frédéric Chopin Institute, Warsaw, 1937.

Catalogues: (*a*) *Exposition: Frédéric Chopin*, Bibliothèque Polonaise, Paris, 1832.

            (*b*) *Exposition de Centenaire: Frédéric Chopin*, Paris, 1949.

Correspondence: (*a*) *Chopin's Letters*, collected by Henry Opieński, trans. E. L. Woynich, Knopf, New York, 1931.

            (*b*) *Correspondence de Frédéric Chopin*, B. Sydow, with Suzanne and Denise Chainaye, 3 vols, Éditions Richard Masse, Paris, 1956–64.

*   *   *   *   *

Binental, Leopold, *Chopin*, Paris, 1934; *Chopin (His Creative Life and His Art)*, Warsaw, 1937; *Chopin: Documents and Souvenirs from His Homeland*, trans. A. Guttry, Leipzig, 1932.

Bory, Robert, *La vie de Chopin par l'image*, Geneva, 1949.

Bronarski, Ludwik, *Chopin et l'Italie*, Lausanne, 1947; *Études sur Chopin*, Lausanne, 1944.

Chainaye, Suzanne and Denise, *Du quoi vivait Chopin?*, Paris, 1951.

Chybinski, Adolf, *Fryderyk Chopin*, Warsaw, 1910.

Ganche, Édouard, *Dans le Souvenir de Frédéric Chopin*, Paris, 1925.

Harasowski, Adam, *The Skein of Legends round Chopin*, MacLellan, Glasgow, 1967.

Hedley, Arthur, *Chopin*, J. M. Dent & Sons, London, 1947 (rev. ed., 1963).

Hoesick, Ferdinand, *Chopin (Life and Work)*, Warsaw, 1904–11.

Jachimecki, Zdzisław, *Fryderyk Chopin*, Cracow, 1927.

Karlowicz, Mieczysław, *Souvenirs inédits de Chopin*, trans. Laure Disière, Paris, 1904.

Kobylanska, Krystyna, *Chopin in His Homeland* and *Chopin Abroad*, Polish Music Publishers, 1955 and 1959.

Lissa, Zofia, *Chopin im Lichte des Briefwechsels von Verlegern seiner Zeit gesehen*, Fontes Artis Musicae, Kassel, 1960–2.

BIBLIOGRAPHY

Mirska, Maria, *Szlakiem Chopina* (On the Track of Chopin), Warsaw, 1935.

Niecks, Frederick, *Frederick Chopin as Man and Musician*, London, 1888.

Sydow, Bronisław, *Bibliografia Chopina*, Warsaw, 1949; *Almanach Chopinowski 1949*, Warsaw, 1949.

Szulc, Marceli Antoni, *Fryderyk Chopin (and His Compositions)*, Poznań, 1873.

Weinstock, Herbert, *Chopin*, New York, 1949.

Zagiba, Franz, *Chopin und Wien*, Vienna, 1951.

Zimmermann, Ewald, 'Probleme der Chopin-Edition,' *Die Musikforschung*, XIV, 2, Kassel, 1961.

'The Book of the First International Musicological Congress devoted to the works of Frederick Chopin', Polish Scientific Publishers, Warsaw, 1960.

INDEXES

Indexes

1. WORKS ARRANGED IN CATEGORIES

Pianoforte Solo

SONGS, Op. 74

DUET FOR 2 PIANOFORTES

CHAMBER MUSIC

PIANOFORTE AND ORCHESTRA

LOST WORKS

2. WORKS WITH OPUS NUMBERS

3. WORKS WITHOUT OPUS NUMBERS

For the 'Deux valses mélancoliques', see **35**.

For nicknamed compositions, and for Wessel's dubbed titles, see General Index, under Nicknamed Compositions, and Appendix IV.

4. GENERAL INDEX

The numbers in this index are item numbers, not page numbers